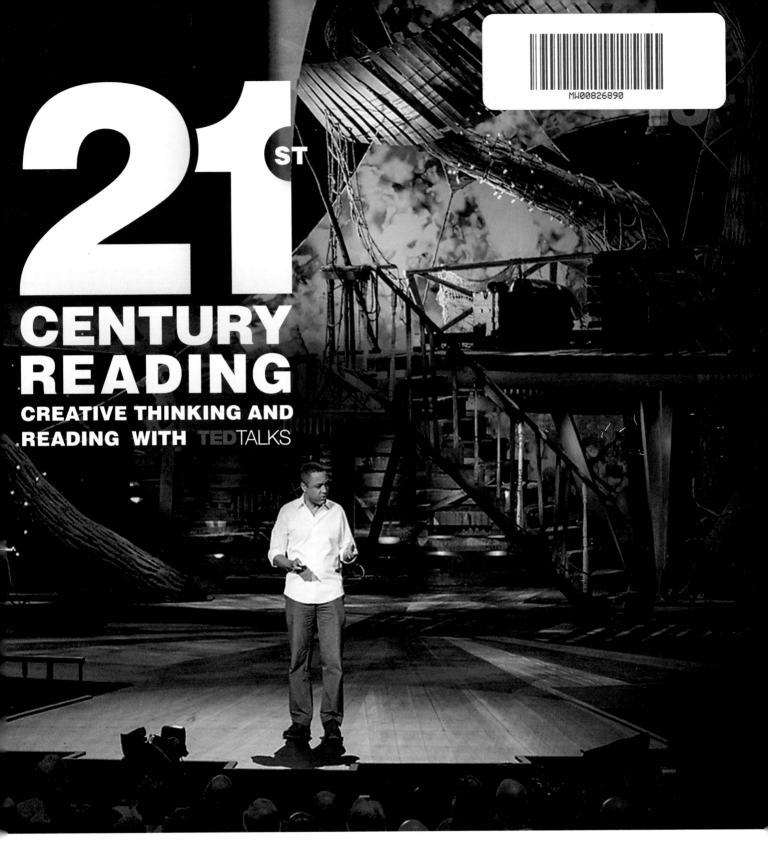

21ST CENTURY READING

CREATIVE THINKING AND READING WITH TED TALKS

Laurie Blass – Mari Vargo – Ingrid Wisniewska – Colleen Sheils

NATIONAL
GEOGRAPHIC
LEARNING

CENGAGE
Learning

Australia • Brazil • Japan • Korea • Mexico • Singapore • Spain • United Kingdom • United States

21st Century Reading Teacher's Guide 3
Creative Thinking and Reading with
TED Talks

Laurie Blass

Mari Vargo

Ingrid Wisniewska

Colleen Sheils

Publisher: Andrew Robinson

Executive Editor: Sean Bermingham

Associate Development Editor: Michelle Harris

Director of Global Marketing: Ian Martin

Product Marketing Manager: Anders Bylund

Media Researcher: Leila Hishmeh

Director of Content and Media Production:
    Michael Burggren

Production Manager: Daisy Sosa

Senior Print Buyer: Mary Beth Hennebury

Cover and Interior Designer:
    Brenda Carmichael

Cover Image: John McWhorter:
    ©James Duncan Davidson/TED

Composition: SPi Global

Teacher Guide
ISBN 13: 978-1-305-26633-9

National Geographic Learning/Cengage Learning
20 Channel Center Street
Boston, MA 02210
USA

Cengage Learning is a leading provider of customised learning solutions with office locations around the globe, including Singapore, the United Kingdom, Australia, Mexico, Brazil and Japan. Locate our local office at **international.cengage.com/region**

Cengage Learning products are represented in Canada by Nelson Education Ltd.

Visit National Geographic Learning online at **NGL.Cengage.com**
Visit our corporate website at **www.cengage.com**

Printed in the United States of America
Print Number: 01   Print Year: 2015

CONTENTS

UNIT WALKTHROUGH

21st Century Reading develops core academic language skills and incorporates 21st Century themes and skills such as global awareness, information literacy, and critical thinking.

Each unit of the Student Book has three parts:

- **Lesson A:** Students read about a 21st Century topic.
- **Lesson B:** Students view a TED Talk which expands upon the topic in Lesson A.
- **Project:** Students explore the topic further by completing a collaborative research project.

1

Each unit begins with an outline of the learning goals.

2

Think and Discuss questions help to raise learners' interest in the unit theme and activate prior knowledge.

3

Lesson A focuses on a reading passage that provides background and context for the TED Talk in Lesson B.

4

Pre-reading activities introduce key terms and content that learners will encounter in the reading passage, and develop previewing skills such as skimming and making predictions.

5 Reading texts are accompanied by glossaries to aid comprehension of lower frequency items that students may be unfamiliar with.

6 **Infographics**, including maps, captions, charts, and graphs, develop learners' visual literacy—their ability to decode graphic information effectively.

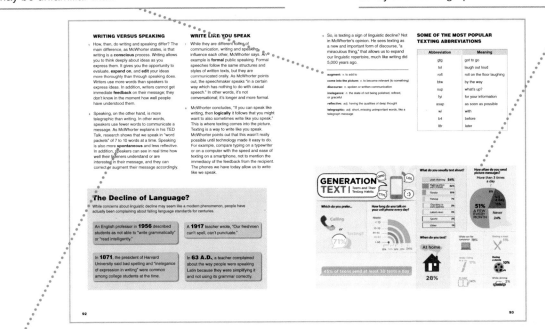

7 Useful academic words and phrases are highlighted in bold and provide the basis for vocabulary building activities later in the lesson.

8 Reading skill tasks focus on key reading strategies such as identifying main and supporting ideas, and understanding cause/effect relationships.

9 Post-reading tasks incorporate graphic organizers, such as sketch maps, Venn diagrams, and timelines in order to help students visualize and understand key concepts.

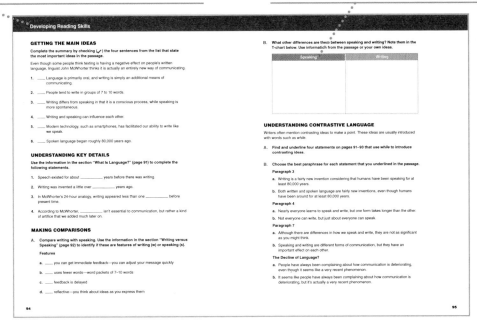

10 Vocabulary building tasks focus on the academic words and phrases highlighted in the passage. All target vocabulary is listed at the back of the student book.

11 Meaning from Context tasks help learners to understand idiomatic and colloquial expressions.

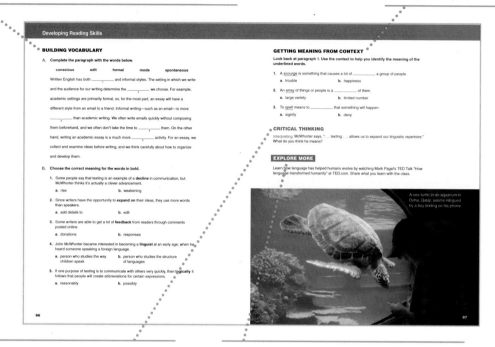

12 Critical Thinking questions encourage students to analyze, evaluate, and apply ideas to their own experience, as well as synthesizing ideas from the reading and the talk.

13 Explore More sections provide suggestions for further reading or viewing—such as related TED Talks and National Geographic articles.

14 Lesson B focuses on the key ideas in a TED Talk that relate to the overall unit theme.

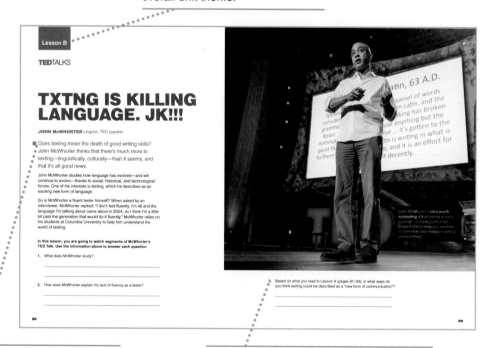

15 A short reading passage provides background information about the speaker.

16 Comprehension questions check students' understanding of the speaker's background.

17 A previewing task typically features a short excerpt from the TED Talk together with questions helping students to predict the main theme.

18 The adapted TED Talks are often divided into two parts, each with associated activities. These parts are also noted in the video transcripts at the back of the Student Book.

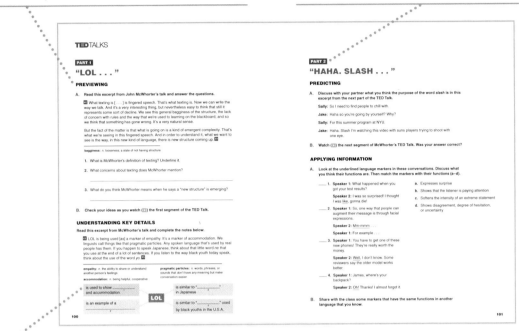

19 A range of visuals are incorporated to summarize key points of the talk and also to preview subject-specific terminology.

20 Guided comprehension tasks focus on the speaker's main ideas, and language he/she uses to convey those ideas.

21 Each unit concludes with a project-based activity which brings together ideas from the unit in a productive task.

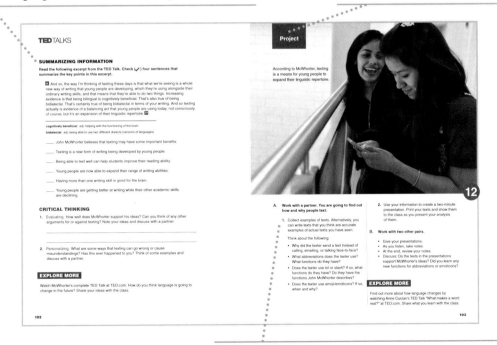

22 **Projects** take the form of research assignments, short presentations, interviews, etc. The Teacher's Guide provides advice for teachers in terms of structuring the project and also suggests functional language to pre-teach before students begin the task.

Series Components

An **Audio CD** features narrations of each reading passage and TED speaker profile. These are highlighted by a (⌒) icon in the Student Book.

A **DVD** accompanying the series contains each adapted TED Talk. Each talk can also be viewed online (visit NGL.Cengage.com/21centuryreading). Viewing activities are highlighted by a (▶) icon in the Student Book.

A photocopiable **TED Talk Summary Worksheet** is provided on page 10 of this Teacher's Guide. This can be used to aid students' comprehension of the TED Talks featured in the Student Book, or those recommended as extension activities.

Annotated Video Transcripts for each TED Talk can be found on pages 71–95 of this Teacher's Guide. These provide explanations of language items and cultural references that may be unfamiliar to students.

Other components in the series include:

- an interactive Student eBook
- an interactive Teacher's eResource that can be used as a presentation tool in class
- an **Assessment CD-ROM** containing ExamView® question banks for teachers who want to create customized tests or give students additional language practice

WELCOME TO 21ST CENTURY READING!

Globalization and the internet are changing the way students learn. Today's young adult and adult ESL/EFL learners need to develop not only core academic English skills such as reading, viewing, and vocabulary skills, but also essential global and cross-cultural awareness, creative and critical thinking skills, and information and media literacies.

In **21st Century Reading**, motivating speakers and innovative content from TED— and its focus on **ideas worth spreading**—provide an exciting opportunity to inspire learners as they develop these essential skills.

The main objective of **21st Century Reading** is to enable learners to understand and respond to ideas and content in English, by reading articles adapted for level and viewing related TED talks. The focus is on the key ideas of each text and talk—and the language that the writer or speaker uses to convey those ideas. In most cases, the TED Talk has been abridged to focus on two or three segments that best represent the speaker's key ideas.

As learners progress through the series, they develop essential reading and vocabulary skills, such as scanning quickly for specific information, making connections between main and supporting ideas, and inferring meaning from context. In addition, learners are encouraged to think critically about each text and TED talk, for example by:

- **Analyzing** an article or excerpt in detail in order to identify key points and arguments.
- **Evaluating** evidence to decide how credible, relevant, or sufficient the information is.
- **Reasoning** and justifying solutions to a problem, based on logical conclusions.
- **Inferring** what a writer or speaker is saying indirectly, and interpreting figurative language.
- **Synthesizing** ideas from more than one source in order to make a judgment or conclusion.
- **Predicting** what will happen, either later in the text or at a future time.
- **Reflecting** on a writer's/speaker's ideas and applying those ideas to other contexts.

We hope that you—and your students—enjoy your journey through **21st Century Reading**, and that along the way you discover many ideas worth spreading!

Name: _____ Class: _____

TED Talk Summary Worksheet

Unit: _____   Video Title: _____

Speaker: _____

What information do you learn about the speaker and his/her background?

_____

_____

_____

Summarize the main idea of the talk in one sentence.

_____

What supporting details or examples does the speaker use to support his/her idea?

_____

_____

_____

How does the speaker engage the audience? For example, using images, charts, humor, actions, etc.

_____

_____

_____

What is your opinion of the talk? What words or phrases would you use to describe it?

_____

_____

_____

What language in the video was new to you? Make a note of three words or phrases that the speaker used. Write a sentence or definition for each one.

_____

_____

_____

HIDDEN MIRACLES

UNIT OVERVIEW

Reading: Students read an interview with a filmmaker who takes time-lapse images of nature.

TED Talk: Photographer Louie Schwartzberg shows wonders of the natural world and talks about how nature is inspiring new technology.

Project: Students research and talk about a kind of technology inspired by nature.

 **Lesson 1A** VIEWING NATURE'S BEAUTY THROUGH A NEW LENS

LESSON OVERVIEW

Aims:
- Read and comprehend an interview with filmmaker Louie Schwartzberg.
- Understand reasons and key details.
- Paraphrasing ideas.

Target Vocabulary: attributed to, challenges, constant, documents, illustrates, issues, primarily, reinforce, specifically, transform

Reading Passage Summary: Students read an interview with Louie Schwartzberg, a filmmaker who is known for his time-lapse images of nature. Schwartzberg shares how he got started in photography as a university student, and how a teacher encouraged him to document the natural world. Schwartzberg has filmed time-lapse images every day, 24 hours a day, for the last 35 years. He explains that time-lapse gives us a new point of view about nature and as a result helps create a connection with nature that people today are lacking.

TEACHING NOTES

THINK AND DISCUSS

This unit introduces photographic technology that can change the way we see, experience, and feel about nature, especially time-lapse photography. Time-lapse photography involves taking images slowly over a long period of time, and then playing them back quickly so viewers can experience something they otherwise wouldn't be able to see. A blooming flower is one typical image captured in time-lapse. As a whole-class activity, elicit some images in nature that would be useful to capture with time-lapse. Then ask students to think about other things in nature that we can't see with our human eyes. Point out that much of nature is made up of microscopic organisms that we can't see at all. In addition, there are events in nature that happen too fast for us to witness (like a bee's wings fluttering). Use question 2 as an opportunity to explain time-lapse photography if students are not already familiar with it. ***Extension:*** Have students work in pairs to search online for more information about time-lapse photography and how it is done.

Think and Discuss

Answers will vary. Possibilities include: **1.** tiny features on insects, grooves on plants, microscopic eggs, etc.; **2.** magnifying glass, telescope, camera with zoom lens, etc.

Pre-reading

A. Guesses will vary. Students read the captions for the actual answers.

B. 1. The passage is about filmmaker Louie Schwartzberg, known for his time-lapse photographs of nature.; **2.** Taken at a slow speed, time-lapse photography picks up details on plants and animals that the human eye cannot.; **3.** Answers will vary.; **4.** c

Getting the Main Ideas

The following should be checked: 1, 3, 4.

Understanding Reasons

Reasons should appear in the following order: c, d, e, b

Understanding Key Details

A. His Process: a, f; **His Start:** b, d; **His Beliefs:** c, e

B. Answers will vary. Possibilities include:

His Process: uses time-lapse, slow-motion, and aerial photography; best known for time-lapse; focuses mostly on flowers; employs survival techniques when shooting

His Start: documented anti-war protests; learned about lighting, composition, color, contrast; began thinking about having a creative and sustainable life

His Beliefs: wants to share how cool nature is; feels it's important to engage young people with nature; people should know how interconnected nature and humans actually are; more attention should be given to bee colony collapse disorder

Paraphrasing

Answers will vary. Possibilities include: **1.** The filming that I've done over the last 35 years has been edited into 12 hours of video.; **2.** You learn to appreciate life more when your mind opens.; **3.** I have the same core experience again and again.

Building Vocabulary

A. 1. challenges; **2.** primarily; **3.** illustrates; **4.** specifically

B. 1. a; **2.** a; **3.** b; **4.** a; **5.** b; **6.** b

Getting Meaning from Context

1. He means that photography has given him a way to share his ideas and opinions.; **2.** "Nature deficit disorder" describes a human disconnect from nature. It is considered to be a problem especially with inner-city youth who have little or no opportunity to have direct contact with nature.

Critical Thinking

1. Interpreting. Answers will vary. He means that both explorers and artists are by nature curious, and this is what motivates them. While they take different approaches to how they explore this curiosity, ultimately they share the goal of wanting to understand nature more and teach others about it.
2. Reflecting. Answers will vary.

PRE-READING

A. Give students a few minutes to look at the pictures. Tell them to guess what they think they are seeing in each photo before reading the caption to check their answers. Then elicit a quick class discussion to hear what surprised students about the pictures. *Extension:* Ask students to share their overall impressions of how seeing something so close up makes them feel. Or have students work in pairs to discuss which picture they think is the most interesting and why.

B. Have students work individually to complete the activity. Point out for question 1 they should read or skim the first paragraph, which is the introduction. For question 3, note that the sentences in bold are the questions that the interviewer asks.

DEVELOPING READING SKILLS

Getting the Main Ideas: Have students read the entire passage, either silently or while listening to the narrated passage on the audio. Have them identify the main points individually before checking answers in pairs. Point out that students should check three statements.

UNDERSTANDING REASONS

Explain that the reasons connected to each idea in the passage are not directly connected through terms like *that's why*, *because*, and *so*. Instead, students must infer the connections based on the content and context in the reading passage. Have students match the ideas with the reasons individually before checking answers as a class. **Extension:** Have students work in pairs to find other ideas and reasons in the passage. Ask each student to present an idea to their partner, for which the partner must find a reason. For example, Schwartzberg says part of his mission is to share how cool nature is. The reason for this mission is that many young people these days have "nature deficit disorder."

UNDERSTANDING KEY DETAILS

A. Explain that a concept map is useful for helping to organize key information in a reading. Have students work alone to complete the activity before checking their answers in pairs. Point out that students only need to focus on the bubbles right now, not the lines below. Make sure students understand that "His process" refers to the way or style in which Schwartzberg does his work. One common use of the noun *process* is to describe an artist's style of working or creating.

B. Ask students to add their ideas on the lines in the boxes below the bubbles in the concept map. Have students work individually before sharing their answers in pairs. Then elicit their ideas for a class discussion. Draw a concept map on the board with the details students come up with.

PARAPHRASING

Explain that *paraphrasing* means to put something in your own words, or different words from the author's. It is a useful tool when summarizing content, as well as when collecting research for a presentation or report. Give students a few minutes to work alone to paraphrase the sentences. Tell them to go back to the reading to look at the sentences nearby if they are uncertain about meaning. Have students compare answers in pairs. Then elicit some examples. Make sure students understand that answers will vary since they are each saying it in their own words; however, the general ideas should be the same. **Extension:** Have students practice paraphrasing more sentences from the passage. Ask partners to each choose a sentence from the reading. Then have both partners paraphrase and compare their general ideas.

BUILDING VOCABULARY

A. Have students complete Exercise A individually before checking answers as a class. While both *primarily* and *specifically* are adverbs used to emphasize a point, *primarily* is used to point out a main idea, while *specifically* is used to point out a precise detail.

B. Have students complete Exercise B individually before checking answers in pairs. The noun *issue* refers to an important topic, often something that is a problem. When we use the word *issues* to discuss an individual, it refers to personal problems. Students may be familiar with the noun *document*, to refer to a record of written information or evidence, usually of an official nature. Explain that the verb *document* is also about making a record of something, but it is not limited to writing.

GETTING MEANING FROM CONTEXT

Explain that getting meaning from context involves looking at Schwartzberg's reply to the question being asked by the interviewer. Have students complete questions 1 and 2 individually before checking answers as a class. **Extension:** Have students work in pairs to go online and learn more about "nature deficit disorder." Then have them paraphrase what they learned and report back to another pair.

CRITICAL THINKING

Encourage students to give reasons and examples to support their answers. *Experts* are team members with specialized skills that are key for the project. *Organizers* are the members who help the team plan and time-manage to finish a project on time. *Experimenters* are the creative members who try different options. **Extension:** To encourage more discussion on the topic, ask: *What's a memorable team project that you worked on? Why was the team successful or not successful?* Have students discuss their answers in pairs.

1. Interpreting Give students time to think about their answers before completing the activity. Then have them share their ideas in pairs before eliciting a class discussion. Schwartzberg sees the process of scientists and artists as different, but what's the same is the motivation of curiosity and the ultimate goal of educating others about the natural world. **Extension:** Have students work in pairs to make a Venn diagram while discussing the differences and similarities in question 1.

2. Reflecting Have students work in pairs. Tell them to give as much description as possible and to give reasons for how their perspectives changed. If time permits, have students go online to find the images they are describing.

EXPLORE MORE

Louie Schwartzberg has given three TED Talks. In the interview in the passage, he touches on his concern about bee colony collapse disorder, which he elaborates further on in his TED Talk, "The hidden beauty of pollination." Note that this is not the same TED Talk in Lesson B.

Lesson 1B HIDDEN MIRACLES OF THE NATURAL WORLD

LESSON OVERVIEW

Aims:

• Watch and understand a talk about what we can learn from seeing nature in a new way.
• Connect main ideas and details.
• Predicting potential uses of time-lapse technology.

TED Talk Summary: In his TED Talk, Schwartzberg shows both time-lapse and high-speed photography images and talks about how they can help change our perspective about the world and our connection to each other and nature. From an aerial of (human) air and sea traffic, to a close-up of the tiniest of organisms living on our eyelashes, Schwartzberg's images open up our understanding of the world. He also talks about how we can learn from creatures like the spider and the dragonfly to create new technologies. An annotated transcript for the edited TED Talk is on page 70–71 of this Teacher's Guide.

TEACHING NOTES

The paragraph and questions introduce Schwartzberg further. Tell students to use the background information that they learned about him in Lesson A, along with the information on page 18, to answer the questions. Make sure that students understand that Schwartzberg's main goal is not only to connect people to nature but to motivate them to protect the planet and the environment. *Extension:* Ask students to write a paragraph or one-page essay about their own relationship with nature. At the end of the lesson, after students have watched the TED Talk and seen Schwartzberg's time-lapse images, have them revisit their writing and see if any of their thoughts or feelings have changed. Ask them to think about whether they want to change their relationship with nature or not.

PART 1

PREVIEWING

A. Have students work individually to read the excerpt and complete the activity. Note that they will read the paragraph with some key words missing. If this confuses students, have them do Exercise B first and then come back to A. Have students share their predictions in pairs.

B. Have students work individually to complete the paragraph before comparing answers in pairs. Explain that their answers may vary, but to check if these words communicate similar ideas or not. Both synonyms and similarly themed answers can work. For example, the answer to item 1 is *surrounded*, but other words that may work include *intrigued* and *fascinated* even though they don't have the same meaning. Make sure students understand that the activity is about finding a word that fits, with which the sentences will still make sense. Play the video and have students compare their guesses with what Schwartzberg actually says. Ask them whether the words were similar or similarly themed.

UNDERSTANDING MAIN IDEAS

Have students work alone to check the main ideas of the first part of the TED Talk. Check answers as a class, eliciting a summary of what Schwartzberg is saying. Elicit what item 4 is referring to: high-speed photography. *Extension:* Have students work individually or in pairs to paraphrase the following line from the talk: "And I love to use film to take us on a journey through portals of time and space, to make the invisible visible, because what that does, it expands our horizons, it transforms our perception, it opens our minds and touches our heart."

1. Living in nature with few distractions from modern life and lots of time encouraged Schwartzberg to begin his time-lapse photography, which has since become his life's work.; 2. He hopes his work will help people find happiness in nature and move them to protect and sustain the planet.

PART 1

Previewing

A. Answers will vary. The film shows us scenes from nature that we have likely never seen, especially microscopic images and videos of events that are slow to happen.

B. Guesses will vary. Actual answers are:
1. surrounded; 2. journey; 3. expands; 4. opens

Understanding Main Ideas

The following should be checked: 2, 4.

Connecting Main Ideas and Details

A. The answers are:

the restless movement of humanity: d, h
the planet as a single organism: i, e, j
nature's ingenious devices: b, a, c, f, g

B. 1. A dragonfly can hover, fly backwards, and even move its four wings in different directions at the same time.; 2. Hovercrafts or robotic flyers that help us explore and learn about remote places.

Critical Thinking

Predicting. Answers will vary. Possibilities include collecting data to learn more about nature, trends connected to human evolution, medical mysteries, among others.

PART 2

Predicting

Guesses will vary. Actual answers are: 1. c; 2. b; 3. d; 4. a

Understanding Key Details

1. thinner, stronger; 2. diseases, clear (clogged), repair

CONNECTING MAIN IDEAS AND DETAILS

A. Have students look over the mind map and answer choices. If necessary, play the video again as students work individually to complete the activity. Note that item a., air flow, refers to the dragonfly, not to the movement of the clouds.

B. Explain that students should use their mind maps to answer the questions in Exercise B. Have students work individually before checking answers in pairs. *Extension:* Ask students to share with a partner which image in the first part of the TED Talk surprised them the most. Did it change their perspective on anything? Ask them to explain.

CRITICAL THINKING

Give students a few minutes to think about their ideas before having a class discussion. Schwartzberg shows us how time-lapse can be used to plot global traffic, which is one practical application. Other ideas include documenting the movement of animals that we otherwise don't see very often, such as nocturnal animals or animals that are very small, as well as the growth of rare plants that are in hard-to-reach parts of the world. It lets us observe and gather important information without disrupting the environment.

PART 2

PREDICTING

Have students work in pairs to examine the pictures closely and complete the activity. Ask pairs to share their guesses with the class and give reasons for them. Or take a class poll to see what the majority of the class thinks each image is. Then play the video. Tell students to check their answers as they watch. *Extension:* Elicit what other things Schwartzberg showed in pictures: a caterpillar's mouth (pages 10–11), the egg of a butterfly (pages 12–13), a mite on a human eyelash, a flea.

UNDERSTANDING KEY DETAILS

Have students work individually to complete the activity before checking answers as a class. Note that the sentences are paraphrases of what Schwartzberg says in his TED Talk. As a result, there may be some small discrepancies in answers depending on how students paraphrase. For example, Schwartzberg talks about how nano devices might be able to *clean clogged arteries*. Another possible choice of words is *unclog arteries*.

Encourage students to search online for some clips of *Mysteries of the Unseen World*. This National Geographic movie shows us images of microscopic life taken with new technology.

 **Project**

RESEARCHING FOR A PRESENTATION ON BIOMIMICRY

PROJECT OVERVIEW:

Aims
- Students research in pairs about a form of technology inspired by something in nature.
- Students watch a TED Talk and give a presentation about the technology introduced in it.
- Students listen to each other's reports and discuss which technology is the most interesting and why.

Summary: Students choose a kind of technology inspired by nature and give a presentation about it to their classmates.

Materials: computer, Internet access, presentation software

Language Support:

Presentation language: *Today I am going to introduce . . . ; Let me first explain . . . ; Let's next talk about . . .*

TEACHING NOTES

PREPARATION

Have students work in pairs. Ask them to go to TED.com and look at the summaries of each of the talks. Monitor students' choices so there are a variety of technologies being presented. Tell them to watch the TED Talk and take notes on the technology, what it does, and how it was inspired by nature. Encourage them to use the questions on page 23 as a guide in their research. Remind them to paraphrase as they research. Note the "Language Support" phrases above on the board and review them before students begin the activity.

DURING THE PROJECT

After pairs watch the TED Talk and gather information, give them time to create their reports. Point out that they can have pictures and/or video to support their presentations, if possible. Remind them that their goal is to present the technology as something interesting. Monitor as pairs prepare their presentations, and give assistance or feedback when necessary. Give students a few minutes to practice their presentations before finding two other pairs to present to. Make sure pairs are not presenting to each other about the same project. Tell all students to listen carefully and take notes while others present.

AFTER THE PROJECT

Have groups discuss each other's presentations. Ask them to decide which technology they found the most interesting and why. Have students comment on what was convincing or persuasive in the presentations they saw. If time permits, have a class discussion about the various technologies to elicit students' thoughts and impressions.

Have students work in pairs to find out about more interesting projects and technologies inspired by nature.

SLEEP MATTERS

UNIT OVERVIEW

Reading: Students read about problems that arise from not getting enough sleep.

TED Talk: Media mogul Arianna Huffington talks about how sleep affects success.

Project: Students research more about and present on a sleep-related topic.

 **SLEEP MATTERS**

LESSON OVERVIEW

Aims:
- Read and comprehend an article about the negative effects of sleep deprivation.
- Identify main ideas, reasons and effects.
- Understand statistics and infographics.

Target Vocabulary: acknowledged, apparently, consequences, crucial, injury, institute, investigation, legal, medical, ultimately

Reading Passage Summary: Students read about how our modern lifestyles keep us from regarding sleep as important, and the dangerous consequences of this. We have information, entertainment, and food available to us at all hours now, and this means that we are staying awake longer than we should. Yet when we don't get enough sleep, our performance level at work, at school, and in life in general suffers. And the consequences can even be dangerous—exhausted people are more likely to cause accidents, some of which can lead to deaths. It's time to rethink our attitude toward sleep, and start getting more of it.

TEACHING NOTES

THINK AND DISCUSS

The unit deals with the theme of sleep and why we need to get more of it. Go over the goals of the unit and elicit the meaning of *current research*. Make sure students understand that it refers to recent studies and published papers, as well as the latest news on the topic. Give students time to think about question 1 before discussing their answers in pairs. Then elicit their ideas about why we need sleep. Ask students to share how much sleep they usually get per night before commenting on what kinds of people may need more sleep than others. The infographic in Lesson A focuses on differences due to age, but other factors such as work or health may also affect how much sleep someone needs. Note that sleep is an easy topic to personalize. Throughout the unit, encourage students to reflect on their own sleep habits and how they might improve them.

Think and Discuss

1. Answers will vary.; **2.** Answers will vary. Infants and young children need many more hours of sleep than adults.

Pre-reading

A. 1. Answers will vary. Sleep is aided by eating well, staying stress-free, not overstimulating yourself at night, etc.; **2.** Answers will vary.; **3.** Answers will vary depending on age. Adults, age 18 or over, need seven to nine hours per night.

B. Predictions will vary. Actual answers are: **1.** We live in a 24/7 culture now where things are available and places are open all the time. Also, people work long hours, which cuts into their sleep time.; **2.** The effects of no sleep include poor performance at work and school. Fatigue is also a major cause of dangerous accidents, such as car crashes.

Getting the Main Ideas

The following should be checked: Modern 24/7 culture is causing more people to suffer from a lack of sleep.; Researchers are learning how sleep deprivation can have a significantly negative effect on performance.

Identifying Reasons and Effects

1. information; **2.** entertainment; **3.** food; **4.** arriving at work early and staying late; **5.** grades; **6.** Pilots; **7.** accidents/crashes; **8.** mistakes

Understanding Statistics

A. 1. 20; **2.** 50; **3.** 5; **4.** 20

B. Answers will vary.

Understanding Infographics

A. 1. Newborns, infants; **2.** Adults; **3.** 8.5 to 9.5; **4.** 11 to 13; **5.** preschoolers

B. 1–2. Answers will vary.

Building Vocabulary

A. 1. crucial; **2.** medical; **3.** injure; **4.** acknowledge; **5.** consequences

B. 1. c; **2.** a, b; **3.** c, d; **4.** a, c; **5.** b

C. Answers will vary.

Getting Meaning from Context

A. 1. a; **2.** c; **3.** e; **4.** f; **5.** d; **6.** g; **7.** b

B. Answers will vary.

Critical Thinking

1. Analyzing. Claim 1: Quote, Stat, Expert; Claim 2: Expert; Claim 3: Stat, Expert; **2. Evaluating.** Answers will vary.

PRE-READING

A. Elicit or explain the meaning of "a good night's sleep." Give students a minute or so to think about and write their answers before discussing their ideas with a partner. Note that answers to question 2 will vary with students' ages. For question 3, ask pairs to raise their hands if they get less sleep than the information shown in the infographic.

B. Note that students are predicting the information, so their answers do not need to be correct. Have students work individually to write their answers before sharing their predictions with a partner. Then have the class brainstorm a list of possible effects that are a result of lack of sleep. Have students check their answers as they read the passage. *Extension:* Point out the passage title: "Are You Sleeping Enough?" Before students read the passage, ask them to work individually to write a paragraph about their own sleep habits and whether they think they get enough sleep or not. Tell them to write about the effect that lack of sleep has on them individually.

DEVELOPING READING SKILLS

Getting the Main Ideas: Have students read the entire passage, either silently or while listening to the narrated passage on the audio. Have them answer the questions individually. Make sure students understand that the first sentence at the top is the first part of the summary and they are choosing the next two sentences in the summary. Check answers as a class. Elicit or explain that all of the incorrect answers are supporting details. Point out that each is a statistic or piece of information that supports the overall thesis. *Extension:* Ask students to work in pairs to brainstorm some examples of a 24/7 culture. Have each pair share their ideas with the class. Some examples include: TV shows are on all the time, online shopping is possible any time of the day, fast-food restaurants never close, etc.

IDENTIFYING REASONS AND EFFECTS

Explain that it is a useful way to organize the information in a text, especially when there are reasons and effects. If necessary, explain the difference between "reason and effect" and "cause and effect" or "reason and result." Cause and effect and reason and result usually have direct correlations, meaning that this specific cause created that specific effect. In the case of the activity, "reasons and effects" is a more general grouping of important information in the article about sleep deprivation. There are reasons for sleep deprivation, and there are effects of sleep deprivation, and both are discussed in the article. Have students work individually to complete the summary map before checking answers in pairs. *Extension:* Have students extend the summary map to include their own personal reasons for sleep deprivation.

UNDERSTANDING STATISTICS

A. Give students a few minutes to complete Exercises A and B individually before checking answers in pairs. Then have students discuss their answers to B with their partners.

B. Ask students to think about their own countries and cultures and how sleep is regarded in modern times. Tell them to share examples of typical sleep deprivation with their partners. *Extension:* Have a class discussion about sleep deprivation around the world. Ask students to share with the class what the attitude toward sleep is in their own countries and how they think sleep deprivation affects people the most.

UNDERSTANDING INFOGRAPHICS

A. Have students work individually to complete the activity before checking answers in pairs. *Extension:* Ask students to think again about their home countries and cultures. Tell them to discuss with their partners any differences with the information in the infographic.

B. Give students a few minutes to think about their answers before having them discuss in pairs. For question 1, an adult's need for sleep may change with their job type, age, or health, for example. A person who has an illness will likely need more sleep. Some jobs require people to stay up all night and sleep during the day. For question 2, ask students to think about what more they want to know, and what they think would improve the infographic.

BUILDING VOCABULARY

A. Have students complete Exercise A individually before checking answers as a class. Point out that the paragraph is a summary of the passage. When we *acknowledge* something, we recognize it to be true. The author of the article is asking us to acknowledge that sleep deprivation is a serious problem.

B. Have students complete Exercise B individually before checking answers as a class. Explain that *institute* is often used to refer to an organization, but it can also refer to a school with a specific focus of study, such as the Institute of Design. An *investigation* involves both research and examination. *Extension:* Have students work individually to write new sentences using the vocabulary words.

GETTING MEANING FROM CONTEXT

A. Give students a few minutes to go back to the reading to find each phrase and complete the activity. Tell them to look at context, or how the phrase is used in the sentence. Check answers as a class. Note that the noun *shut-eye* is a synonym for *sleep*. It's used more often when talking about needing sleep or not getting enough of it: *I only got three hours of shut-eye last night*. *Extension:* Ask students to work in pairs to make a list of synonyms for *sleep*. Some examples include: *nap, doze, shut-eye, beauty sleep*, etc.

B. Write "change your perspective" and its definition on the board (understand something in a different way). Explain that when you change your perspective about something, it means that you previously thought differently about it. Tell students that they can talk about something big or small, but it must involve a change in their thinking.

CRITICAL THINKING

1. Analyzing. Give students a few minutes to go back to the reading and find the support for each claim. If necessary, review the meaning of *quote*, *statistic*, and *information from experts*. Point out that some claims will have more than one kind of support. Check answers as a class, asking students to identify the stat, quote, or expert information in the passage.

2. Evaluating. Elicit a class discussion and ask students to share their thoughts about the article. Is it convincing? How could it be more convincing? Has it changed their perspectives about anything? *Extension:* Have students share with a partner how the article has changed their perspective about sleep, and why.

EXPLORE MORE

Tell students to try to find information that will further support the writer's claims or change their perspective about something.

LESSON OVERVIEW

Aims:
- Watch and understand a talk about how sleep can help us reach success.
- Recognize main ideas.
- Understand a classification and metaphors.
- Identify the speaker's message.

TED Talk Summary: In her TED Talk, media entrepreneur Arianna Huffington speaks about the mistaken attitude that less sleep is better for productivity. She talks about how men in business commonly brag about how little sleep they get, yet she points out that this may be the reason for many of the problems in the world. Speaking at TED Women, she addresses the audience of women directly to say that changing their attitudes about sleep will lead them to better ideas, better productivity, and a better world. She insists that women will be the ones to lead this change in thinking about sleep. An annotated transcript for the edited TED Talk is on page 73–74 of this Teacher's Guide.

TEACHING NOTES

The passage introduces Huffington, who is considered one of the most influential people in the world. A media entrepreneur and author, Huffington's online journal *The Huffington Post* is one of the most-visited sites on the Internet. She has both wealth and power, but after having an accident due to sleep deprivation, her thoughts on what really aids success have changed. She now believes that our well-being as individuals is also a key factor, and that sleep is a significant part of this.

PART 1

PREVIEWING

A. Have students read the excerpts individually before discussing in pairs. Note that the excerpts are from the very opening of her talk. If necessary, elicit or explain the meanings of *dormant, fainted, stitches*. Students should recognize that Huffington is explaining an experience that changed her perspective on sleep. She used to believe that work was more important than sleep, but after a fatigue-related injury, her thinking changed.

B. Have students check their answers to Exercise A as they watch the video.

UNDERSTANDING MAIN IDEAS

A. Have students work individually to read the excerpt and complete the activity before checking their answers in pairs. **Extension:** Ask students to offer their ideas about why Huffington specifically spoke to medical doctors and scientists to learn about sleep and productivity.

B. Have students discuss their answers in pairs. Huffington uses the terms *more productive*, *more inspired*, and *more joyful*. Ask students to give examples of what they think she means for each of these. **Extension:** Have students share in pairs how their own lives might benefit if they were more productive, more inspired, and more joyful. Then ask them to discuss whether they think getting more sleep will accomplish this or not.

UNDERSTANDING A CLASSIFICATION

Students are asked here to study further about a topic mentioned in the talk: Type A personalities. The passage explains about personality types, and what Type A is. Generally, people who are ambitious, aggressive workers, and often highly productive are considered Type A. Huffington knows that many of the people in her audience are Type A, and she also knows that this type, while very productive, has a hard time slowing down. These are the people who will think sleep is not important, and it's their minds that she wants to change.

PART 2

UNDERSTANDING METAPHORS

A. Give students a minute to read the excerpt and complete the activity.

B. Play the video. Ask students to check their ideas as they watch. Elicit a more detailed explanation of the metaphor. Huffington uses the metaphor of the *Titanic* hitting the iceberg to give an example of a disaster that was actually avoidable if someone had been more alert. She is not saying that the captain of the *Titanic* was sleep-deprived, but she is saying that when we are sleep-deprived, we make similar, disastrous mistakes that are otherwise avoidable. Elicit the

1. Huffington was born in Athens, Greece, and went to the University of Cambridge in England.; **2.** media and journalism; **3.** That good heath and balance are also keys to success; **4.** Her news and blog site is one of the most viewed in the world. People are also exposed to her ideas through her articles, her books, and her radio talk shows.

PART 1

Previewing

A. 1. She means that people who are sleep-deprived are not able to have good ideas. By sleeping more, our creativity will thrive. She is referring to the ideas that are inside everyone, which never emerge because we are too tired to be innovative.; **2.** She is explaining why and how she began to fully understand and appreciate the power of sleep.

Understanding Main Ideas

A. c

B. With more sleep, people become more productive, more inspired, and more joyful.

Understanding a Classification

1. Type B because they worry the least; **2.** Answers will vary.; **3.** Answers will vary.; **4.** Type A people are the

most likely to value work over sleep, and therefore not get enough sleep.

PART 2

Understanding Metaphors

A. a

Understanding a Speaker's Message

A. 1. something that demonstrates to others that you are powerful and important; they don't sleep a lot; **2.** She says that the date wasn't very interesting, by which she is trying to illustrate that the man would have been a better date if he had slept more.

B. Her point is that most women are more likely to recognize the power of sleep, and perhaps some major world crises could have been avoided if more well-rested women were in places of power, instead of sleep-deprived men.

Critical Thinking

1. Evaluating. Answers will vary.; **2. Synthesizing.** She offers the same message: Sleep deprivation is hurting global society and is dangerous. She additionally points out the positive side of getting more sleep, most notably how it can actually make us more productive and help us enjoy life more.

---

specific example Huffington gives of this: the financial crisis that hit the U.S. and global stock markets in 2008. *Extension:* Have students work in pairs to brainstorm some other examples of times when no one saw the iceberg coming before the *Titanic* hit it. Or ask them to give an example from their own lives.

UNDERSTANDING A SPEAKER'S MESSAGE

A. Have students work individually to read the excerpt and answer the questions. Then have students share their ideas in pairs. After a few minutes, check answers as a class and elicit a discussion. Note that *virility* actually refers to a man's ability to procreate, or his sex drive. However, it is often used as a metaphor to talk about masculinity and power, which is why a *virility symbol* is something that is supposed to make a man seem more masculine. Sleeping fewer hours than others has become one way to brag about how strong you are in modern times because you can still be productive without a full night's sleep. Huffington says

that this type of bragging is most typical in men. Yet, she points out that these men actually aren't as productive or, as in the case of her date, interesting, as they would be if they slept enough each night.

B. Have students discuss in pairs. If necessary, explain, elicit, or have students do some online research to learn more about Lehman Brothers. Huffington is referring to the 2008 stock market crash that caused a global financial crisis. While clearly Lehman Brothers did not have only male employees, Huffington is saying that the mind-set of the company, to keep pushing forward without taking time to look ahead, is typical of men especially. Her metaphor about the *Titanic* had a similar point, but the Lehman Brothers reference brings it to modern times.

CRITICAL THINKING

1. Evaluating Have students discuss in pairs. Ask them to first share their opinion and then offer some reasons and examples to support it. If time permits, elicit a class discussion.

2. Synthesizing Give students time to go back to the reading passage and review its contents in relation to Huffington's TED Talk. Note that both the talk and the passage support the idea that we should sleep more and that sleep deprivation causes problems and can even be dangerous. While the article offers more research and scientific support for this thesis, Huffington talks about how getting more sleep can make our lives better overall. ***Extension:*** Have students work individually to write a paragraph, or have them talk in pairs about how what they learned in the unit may affect their sleeping habits.

EXPLORE MORE

Gamble's talk is less than five minutes long. She explains how our natural sleep cycle actually includes two hours of restful wake time during the night.

RESEARCHING FOR A PRESENTATION ABOUT SLEEP

PROJECT OVERVIEW:

Aims
- Students work in pairs to research a topic related to sleep.
- Students use what they learned in the unit and in their research to make a presentation.
- Students discuss what they learned from each other's presentations.

Summary: Students choose a sleep-related topic, research it online, and prepare a two-minute presentation. Students review what they learned from each other's presentations and discuss what interested them the most.

Materials: computer, access to the Internet, presentation software

Language Support:

Giving a Presentation: *What I want to talk about first is . . . ; The next point I want to talk about is . . . ; Another interesting point is . . .*

TEACHING NOTES

PREPARATION

Have students work in pairs. Tell them to look over the list of sleep-related topics. Give them a few minutes to discuss what interests them. Tell them to use the background knowledge they acquired during the unit to make their choices. Check each pair's choice to ensure that a variety of topics are being researched. Have pairs go online to find out more about their topics. Tell them to take notes as they research. Note the "Language Support" phrases above on the board and review them before students begin the activity.

DURING THE PROJECT

Explain that each pair will give a two-minute presentation. Tell students to gather the right amount of material to give an informative presentation in two minutes. Point out that they can use pictures, drawings, video, or infographics as visual aids in their presentations. Encourage them to gather real examples, statistics, case studies, stories, and quotes from experts to support their presentations. Monitor as pairs work together and give assistance or feedback when necessary as they prepare their presentation. Give pairs a few minutes to practice their presentations once. Then have pairs present to two other pairs.

AFTER THE PROJECT

Tell students to listen carefully as other pairs present. Ask them to take notes and think of questions for each pair. After all pairs have presented, have groups discuss. Tell students to share what they found interesting and surprising in each other's presentations. Then open the discussion to the entire class. Ask students to share with the class what they learned in the presentations and what they now want to learn more about. ***Extension:*** Have each student comment on how what they learned may affect their own sleeping habits.

EXPLORE MORE

Have students work in pairs to listen to Foster's talk or assign it as homework. Ask students to summarize what Foster says about brain function and sleep.

CYBORG TECH

UNIT OVERVIEW

Reading: Students are introduced to examples of cyborg technology and how each has helped change someone's life.

TED Talk: Neil Harbisson talks about how a cyborg device enhanced his life.

Project: Students research a type of cyborg technology and present about it.

 **Lesson 3A** WE ARE CYBORGS

LESSON OVERVIEW

Aims:
- Read and comprehend an article about cyborg devices helping people change the way they experience the world.
- Understand main ideas and key details.

Target Vocabulary: adapting, advanced, components, data, implanted, mechanical, networks, permanently, removed, utilize

Reading Passage Summary: Students read an article about cyborg technology and how it is changing individual lives. This growing brand of technology is not only improving lives, it's broadening the limits of what humans can do. Yet there is also another side of the discussion that argues that we should not become too dependent on technology for our experiences in the world.

TEACHING NOTES

THINK AND DISCUSS

This unit takes a look at how cyborg technology is changing lives and perhaps expanding our experiences as humans. Cyborg technology refers to a device, usually attached to our bodies, that improves something about the physical way we experience the world. For question 1, have the class brainstorm a list of devices used to improve eyesight and hearing, either low-tech or high-tech. Then ask students to think about how each can improve a person's life. Ask students to also think about how they use technology in their own lives to improve their experiences. For question 2, have students work in pairs to discuss their ideas. *Extension:* Have students work in pairs to design a cyborg device to help people see or hear better. As they go through the unit, ask them to think about whether any of the devices they learn about resemble the one they designed.

Think and Discuss

1. Answers will vary. Possibilities include: glasses, magnifiers, hearing aids, cochlear implants, etc.;
2. Answers will vary. Wearable technology is being further developed to improve our daily lives, and cyborg technology aims to change how we physically experience the world.

Pre-reading

A. Guesses will vary. Actual answers are: **Argus II:** a bionic eye that allows the wearer to see light by connecting the optic nerve to a special type of glasses; **Cochlear implant:** a computer implant in the skull that connects to auditory nerves; **EyeTap:** a device worn over the eyes that blocks out things the wearer doesn't want to see—such as an advertisement—and replaces them with something more interesting.

B. 1. A cyborg is a human whose abilities are improved by advanced technology.; **2.** Answers will vary. Possibilities include: robotic body parts with mobility and superhuman strength, man-made transplant organs, artificial skin, etc.

Getting the Main Ideas

A. b

B. The following should be checked: a, b, d.

Understanding Key Details

A. 1. It has a camera in it that he uses to film what he sees. He uses it to record footage for a documentary.;

2. Hester's bionic eye is actually connected to his optic nerve, whereas Spence's eye is not connected to his optic nerve or brain.; **3.** The cochlear implant helps Chorost hear.; **4.** It helps him block out images that he doesn't want to see, such as advertisements, and replaces them with interesting content, such as an article.

B. He hopes to have transmitters implanted in the ear in his arm in order to be able to hear from it.

Critical Thinking

1. Analyzing. Case explains that the way we've introduced computers and smartphones into our daily lives has made us cyborgs, as both of these devices give us abilities that we otherwise wouldn't have.
2. Evaluating. Answers will vary.

Building Vocabulary

A. 1. mechanical; **2.** network; **3.** adapting; **4.** implant; **5.** removed

B. 1. e; **2.** d; **3.** b; **4.** a; **5.** c

Getting Meaning from Context

1. Arcadiou does not need the ear to help him with a deficiency; instead, he simply wants to add to what his body already has. Perhaps once the ear has the ability to hear, he can be called a cyborg.; **2.** b

Critical Thinking

Evaluating. Answers will vary.

PRE-READING

A. Give students a few minutes to look at the photos and read the captions. Have students work individually to answer the questions before comparing ideas with a partner. Make sure students understand that they are guessing the answers and they do not need to be correct. After students read the article, have them come back and discuss their guesses again.
Extension: Ask pairs to guess which device has changed 300,000 lives (cochlear implant).

B. Give students two minutes to quickly read the first paragraph and answer the questions. Have them check their answers with a partner.

DEVELOPING READING SKILLS

GETTING THE MAIN IDEAS

A. Have students read the entire passage, either silently or while listening to the narrated passage on the audio. Have them work individually to answer the questions for Exercises A and B. Check answers as a class.

B. Ask students to look at the remaining statements and identify which main idea each one supports. Then ask students to offer more evidence from the reading.

UNDERSTANDING KEY DETAILS

A. Give students a few minutes to go back to the reading passage to find the answers. Point out that answering the questions will give students a good chance to practice scanning for specific information. For a challenge, give them one minute to complete the activity. Have them check answers in pairs.

B. Make sure students understand that the question refers to "A Third Ear" (bottom of page 45). Have students work individually to answer the question before checking answers as a class. Ask students to share their opinions about Arcadiou's future plans and use of cyborg technology. *Extension:* Have a class debate about whether changing our bodies like Arcadiou has done is a good idea or not.

CRITICAL THINKING

1. Analyzing. Have students work individually to answer the question before checking answers as a class. Elicit additional examples that support Case's ideas besides smartphones and computers. Some examples include GPS devices, mobile Wi-Fi devices, etc. Write the list of examples on the board and use this to transition into the discussion for question 2.

2. Evaluating. Ask students to think about Case's examples as well as their own. Then have them share their opinions about whether these are good examples of cyborg technology or not. Tell them to decide whether they agree with Case's point or not.

BUILDING VOCABULARY

A. Have students complete Exercise A individually before checking answers in pairs. Individuals who rely on bionics or cyborg technology need a period to adjust to it both physically and mentally. During this period, they *adapt* to the device. In this case, *adapt* means to become accustomed to something new. *Extension:* Have students work in pairs to summarize what the paragraphs teach them about bionics.

B. Have students complete Exercise B individually before checking answers in pairs. A *component* is any part of a larger whole. The term is especially used when talking about mechanical parts. The verb *utilize* is a synonym for *use*, and contains the idea that you are applying something in a practical way.

GETTING MEANING FROM CONTEXT

Have students read the explanation about understanding words in context. Make sure students understand that it's about looking at the words around the unknown word and making an educated guess about its meaning. This skill helps keep the flow of reading, as well as helps when resources like a dictionary are not readily available. Note that students are first asked to discuss the quote before identifying the meaning of the unknown term.

CRITICAL THINKING

Evaluating. If possible, have students discuss in pairs or small groups. Encourage them to make a mind map or list of the pros and cons of cyborg technology. Then have them share their thoughts with the class, and support their opinions with reasons and examples. *Extension:* Ask students to write a paragraph about the kind of cyborg technology that they would like to try. Then have them share their ideas with a partner.

EXPLORE MORE

Encourage students to think more about their own relationship with their smartphones. Ask them to think about how their lives would change without their smartphones. Then ask them to comment on whether they are dependent on their "cyborg technology" or not.

Lesson 3B — I LISTEN TO COLOR

LESSON OVERVIEW

Aims:
- Watch and understand a talk about a cyborg device that altered the way one man experiences the world.
- Understand key details.

TED Talk Summary: In his TED Talk, artist Neil Harbisson explains about his cyborg device, the Eyeborg. He is completely color blind, but his device lets him hear the frequencies of each color he sees. He says that it has not only changed his art, but has enhanced the way he experiences the world. Harbisson shares his own story to show us the great possibilities of using cyborg technology to change us in positive ways. An annotated transcript for the edited TED Talk is on pages 75–76 of this Teacher's Guide.

TEACHING NOTES

The paragraph and questions introduce TED Talk speaker Neil Harbisson and his role as a cyborg activist. Harbisson spends most of his talk sharing details about his device and how it has changed both his art and the way he interacts with the world. *Extension:* Have students work individually to look through the pictures in the unit and write one or two questions about Harbisson's device that they hope are answered in his TED Talk.

PART 1

PREVIEWING

A. Have students work individually to complete the paragraph before comparing answers in pairs. Explain that their answers may vary, but they should check if these words communicate similar ideas or not. Both synonyms and similarly themed answers can work. Make sure students use the definitions in the footnotes to help them understand Harbisson's explanation of the Eyeborg. *Extension:* Have students work in pairs to summarize and paraphrase what Harbisson is saying in the excerpt.

B. Ask students to use the information from Exercise A and the warm-up on the previous pages to answer the question. Remind students that getting meaning from context involves looking at the words around an unknown term. *Extension:* Have students work

individually to write three sentences that each use the term *grayscale*.

C. Have students check their answers to Exercises A and B as they watch. Play the video.

UNDERSTANDING KEY DETAILS

Have students work individually to complete the sentences before checking answers in pairs. *Extension:* If students haven't summarized the content together yet, have them work in pairs to describe in their own words what Harbisson's device does.

UNDERSTANDING A PROCESS

Give students a minute or two to look over the information. Have them work individually to complete the activity before comparing their answers in pairs. Then elicit a paraphrase of each of the steps in the process of the Eyeborg. Ask the class what they think about the device.

PART 2

UNDERSTANDING KEY DETAILS

Give students two minutes to read the paragraph before watching Part 2 of the talk. Then play the video. After students watch, have them work individually to complete the sentences before checking answers in pairs. Tell them to look over Harbisson's color wheel on page 54 to help them with their answers. *Extension:* Have students discuss in pairs what was interesting or surprising to them in the diagram. Ask them to tell each other two sounds that they'd like to know the color of. Tell them to guess what color it would be and why.

CRITICAL THINKING

1. Reflecting. Give students time to think about their answers first before discussing in pairs. Note that Harbisson talks mostly about the advantages of the Eyeborg and how it has changed his life for the better. For the second question, encourage students to work together to brainstorm some possible disadvantages. Then elicit a class discussion to hear students' ideas. *Extension:* Tell students they have a chance to spend a year wearing the Eyeborg. Ask them to discuss in pairs what they'd like to do during that year.

1. Harbisson is color-blind. Since he can't see colors, his artwork lacked colors, too.; **2.** It matches colors with sound, which allows Harbisson to hear a different sound for each color.; **3.** As a cyborg activist, Harbisson helps people who want to become cyborgs, defends the rights of people with cyborg devices, and promotes cyborg research. He also educates the general public on the benefits of cyborg technology. In addition to art, Harbisson is clearly also interested in being active with issues related to cyborg technology.

PART 1

Previewing

A. Guesses will vary. Actual answers are: looks, seeing, sends, hear.

B. Answers will vary. Harbisson is explaining that when he looks around, he only sees white, black, and the various shades of gray in between.

Understanding Key Details

1. hear color; **2.** names, notes; **3.** brain, cyborg

Understanding a Process

1. installed; **2.** sound waves; **3.** travel

PART 2

Understanding Key Details

1. pictures; **2.** notes; **3.** colors; **4.** infrared; **5.** ultraviolet

Critical Thinking

1. Reflecting. Answers will vary. Harbisson's world has become brightened by the sound of all the colors around him. He seems to genuinely enjoy using the Eyeborg. Some drawbacks include possible limitations of the device, for example, perhaps he can't go in water easily. Others might say he is too dependent on the sounds of the device and that it takes away from his natural experiences.

2. Discussion. Answers will vary. Each device is similar to the Eyeborg in certain ways. Spence's bionic eye influences his work and art in a similar way that Harbisson's does. The Argus II provides an alternative for a lost ability as the Eyeborg does for Harbisson. In a similar way, the cochlear implant helps replace a lost ability. And the Eyeborg also changes an existing ability in the same way Mann's EyeTap does.

2. Discussion. Give students time to go back to Lesson A and review the other cyborg technology that they've learned about in the lesson. Tell them to think about Harbisson's cyborg device as they do this. Note that in some ways, each device is similar to the Eyeborg. Explain that students may have different answers. Encourage them to support their opinions with reasons and examples. Have students discuss in pairs. If time permits, elicit a class discussion to hear their ideas as well.

EXPLORE MORE

Harbisson goes into great detail about how he experiences the world with his Eyeborg during his full-length talk. He also talks about how his art, which is made using the technology of the Eyeborg, helps others "see" the world in a new way. *Extension:* Have students listen to the talk and choose their favorite example of how the Eyeborg changes perception.

RESEARCHING FOR A PRESENTATION ON CYBORG TECHNOLOGY

PROJECT OVERVIEW

Aims:
- Students research in pairs about another kind of cyborg technology.
- Students explain the invention to their classmates in a two-minute presentation.
- Students listen and decide which device is the most interesting.

Summary: Students watch a new TED Talk to learn about another example of cyborg technology. They present to classmates and then discuss which technology is the most interesting.

Materials: computer, Internet access, presentation software

Language Support: Showing interest: *Really? That's so interesting; Wow, that's amazing.*

TEACHING NOTES

PREPARATION

Have students work in pairs. Ask them to choose one of the TED Talks listed on page 55. Monitor students' choices so that there is a variety of technologies being presented on. Or assign talks so that the talks are evenly distributed among the pairs. Explain that they should watch the talk, take notes, and then organize a presentation with pictures, video, and information to introduce the invention to other pairs. Encourage students to search online for even more information about the device. Note the "Language Support" phrases above on the board and review them before students begin the activity.

DURING THE PROJECT

Tell partners to take notes individually as they watch the talk. Remind them to use the questions as a guide. Or have partners choose different questions to answer while watching. Monitor as pairs prepare their presentations and give assistance or feedback when necessary. Give students a few minutes to practice their presentations before finding two other pairs. Tell all students to listen carefully and take notes while the other pairs present.

AFTER THE PROJECT

Have pairs discuss what they learned from each other's presentations. Encourage them to debate which device is the most interesting and which is the most useful, giving reasons and examples to support their opinions. Ask students to also discuss which device they think will be the most popular, and which they'd be most likely to use themselves. ***Extension:*** Divide the class into teams based on which TED Talk pairs watched. Then have a class debate about which device is the most useful.

HAPPY PLANET

UNIT OVERVIEW

Reading: Students read about why traditional measurements of a nation's progress might not be so accurate after all.

TED Talk: Statistician Nic Marks introduces his Happy Planet Index for measuring human progress and shares five ways to become happier.

Project: Students create a plan to raise the Happy Planet Index of their local communities.

 **Lesson 4A** THE ROAD TO HAPPINESS?

LESSON OVERVIEW

Aims:
- Read and comprehend an article about why we need to rethink the GNP as a measurement of human progress.
- Link ideas to compare and contrast viewpoints.
- Analyze an argument.
- Understand infographics.

Target Vocabulary: civilization, deconstruction, degradation, desolate, fundamental, invest, promote, worthwhile

Reading Passage Summary: Students read an argument against using a country's gross national product (GNP) to measure progress. Statistician Nic Marks believes it's time to rethink the GNP and to start considering well-being too. He explains that we tend to focus on negative outcomes instead of ways to improve our situation globally. If we think about improvements, we can then focus our time, efforts, and resources on making positive outcomes.

TEACHING NOTES

THINK AND DISCUSS

This unit looks at the abstract concept of happiness and talks about measuring it in concrete terms. The questions on page 56 encourage students to do their own thinking on the topic before reading what others have to say. Give students time to think about their answers before discussing in pairs. After pairs discuss, elicit a class discussion about what students think is important for happiness. Write a mind map on the board with their ideas. Let students refer back to this mind map as they work through the discussion activities in the unit.

PRE-READING

A. Have students look at the photo and read the caption on page 59 before discussing in pairs. Encourage students to brainstorm a list of adjectives that they can use to describe the scene in the picture. Ask if anyone has seen the movie or read the book. If so, elicit more information about *The Road.*

Think and Discuss

1. and 2. Answers will vary.

Pre-reading

A. Answers will vary. The scene is bleak, and the future presented in it is one of desolation. The individuals look fearful, lonely, hungry, and desperate.

B. 1. Robert F. Kennedy says that there are many elements that make up the happiness of the people of a nation that are not being considered in the GNP.; **2.** Answers will vary. Possibilities include: happiness, health, love, etc.

Getting the Main Ideas

1. c; **2.** b; **3.** c; **4.** a

Linking Ideas

1. problems; **2.** solutions; **3.** improve (our situation); **4.** time and resources; **5.** improvements; **6.** dominant; **7.** goal in life; **8.** money; **9.** makes life worthwhile

Analyzing an Argument

A. 1. Marks says that these negative visions stir a fight-or-flight response in us, which often makes us freeze and try to escape the situation, instead of focusing on how to fix it.; **2.** Progress is measured by financial wealth and economic gains, instead of by people's well-being and happiness.

B. The infographic shows that happiness, health, love, and meaning are most important for people, and that wealth is not the first priority.

Understanding Infographics

A. 1. seven; **2.** important; **3.** Happiness; **4.** Health; **5.** fifth

B. 1–3. Answers will vary. Possibilities include: **1.** The people surveyed, even though from many different countries, all tend to value the same things in life.;

There is not a huge difference between the most valued concept and the lowest valued one.; **2.** Some cultures might value something more that isn't on the list of seven.; **3.** What does each of the items on the list actually mean? What items are not on the list that people still value? Why is attractiveness so high?

Building Vocabulary

A. 1. invest, promoting; **2.** degradation; **3.** aspiration; **4.** worthwhile

B. 1. b; **2.** d; **3.** a; **4.** c; **5.** e

C. 1.–2. Answers will vary.

Getting Meaning from Context

1. The term *worst-case scenario* refers to a situation where all negative outcomes happen, such as total environmental disaster that destroys global society as we know it.; **2.** He is referring to efforts to make people help protect and sustain our natural world. Scientists and activists educate the public in order to change their attitude and habits about using the planet's resources.; **3.** When an animal is faced with danger, it either fights its enemy or runs away from it. This is the fight-or-flight response.

Critical Thinking

1. Evaluating. Answers will vary.
2. Questioning. Answers will vary. Possibilities include: Worst-case scenarios in regards to the environment don't motivate us to act to save it.; The GNP is not a well-rounded measurement of progress.; People all over the world value happiness over money, etc.

Explore More

The survey is designed to help companies and organizations measure the happiness of employees.

B. Give students time to read the quote from Kennedy and the first paragraph. Discuss answers as a class. Explain that Robert F. Kennedy was an American politician who was also the brother of President John F. Kennedy. Ask them to skim the information on page 60 to get the main idea of the infographic. Make sure students refer to the footnote that defines GNP. *Extension:* Have students make a mind map of their ideas for question 2. Tell them to refer back to this mind map as they go through the lesson.

DEVELOPING READING SKILLS

GETTING THE MAIN IDEAS

Have students read the entire passage, either silently or while listening to the narrated passage on the audio. Have them work individually to answer the questions before checking answers in pairs.

LINKING IDEAS

Give students one minute to look over the summary chart to recognize what information they need to find. Have students work individually to go back through the reading to complete the chart before checking answers in pairs. Note that most of the answers are verbatim from the reading, but in some cases students may need to paraphrase.

ANALYZING AN ARGUMENT

A. Have students work individually to answer the questions before checking as a class. Ask students to share any examples of post-apocalyptic stories or movies that they've seen. Encourage them to also think about informative environmental messages they've seen that focus primarily on scaring us into action. For question 2, ask students to also discuss whether they agree with Marks or not. *Extension:* Have a class debate about the effectiveness of environmental awareness campaigns or movies that use negative outcomes to scare us into action. Is there any benefit to them? If so, what?

B. Give students a minute to look over the infographic on page 60 and think about the question before writing their answers. Students should notice that wealth is not what people consider the most essential concept for well-being. Note that the next exercise, **Understanding Infographics**, will ask students to look at the infographic in more detail.

UNDERSTANDING INFOGRAPHICS

A. Have students work individually to complete the sentences before checking answers in pairs. Make sure students understand that wealth is five out of a list of seven, which makes it neither the lowest of people's concerns nor the most important. *Extension:* Divide students into seven groups. Ask them to define each of the concepts in more detail and to give some examples of each. Have groups report back to the class.

B. Give students time to work individually to read and think about the questions before discussing answers in pairs. Then elicit a class discussion. Ask students to offer ideas about question 2 based on their own cultural backgrounds.

BUILDING VOCABULARY

A. Have students complete Exercise A individually before checking answers as a class. When a thing is *degraded*, it is falling apart. When a person is *degraded* or acts in a *degrading* way, it refers to being disrespected or behaving disrespectfully. Something that is *worthwhile* is worth the time, effort, or cost that is required to have or accomplish it.

B. Have students complete Exercise B individually before checking answers in pairs. For a challenge, tell students not to use a dictionary but to find the meaning by looking at the word in context in the reading. *Extension:* Have students write sentences using each of the vocabulary words defined in Exercise B.

C. Give students a few minutes to work individually to think about and write their answers before discussing in pairs. Elicit some ideas that students talked about in question 2. *Extension:* Have students work individually to write a one-page essay about their aspirations for their futures over the next ten years. Tell them to use as many vocabulary words as possible in the essay.

GETTING MEANING FROM CONTEXT

Have students work individually to answer the questions before discussing their ideas in pairs. Then check answers as a class.

CRITICAL THINKING

1. Evaluating. Ask students to think about movies they've seen or books they've read about a future world. If students are having trouble thinking of examples, encourage them to think about movies that show the future as a world with exciting technology, such as *Back to the Future, Star Trek,* etc.

2. Questioning. Give students time to go back over the reading passage together to examine the claims made by Marks or the author. Tell them that when they come across one that they don't agree with or might be able to argue, they should write down the claim and their thoughts. Check answers as a class by eliciting claims and students' opinions about them. *Extension:* Have students write a rebuttal to the claim that they disagree with. Give them time to go online and collect support for their opinions.

EXPLORE MORE

At nicmarks.org, students can learn about his various projects in relation to measuring happiness. Note that Marks's TED Talk in Lesson B covers his Happy Planet Index. Information about the Happiness at Work survey is under the Big Ideas section. *Extension:* Instead of having all students find out more about the Happiness at Work survey, divide the class into groups and assign each group one Big Idea on Marks's site to research and report back on.

THE HAPPY PLANET INDEX

LESSON OVERVIEW

Aims:
- Watch and understand a talk about measuring happiness.
- Identify key details.
- Recognize a speaker's message.

TED Talk Summary: In his TED Talk, Nic Marks explains the Happy Planet Index, which he designed as a way to measure which countries are happiest. It is calculated using the ecological footprint of a country, as well as the life expectancy and well-being of its people. For Marks, this is a better measure of progress than GNP. Marks reveals that the country with the highest HPI in the world (at the time of his talk) is Costa Rica. He also goes into detail about the five habits that happy people have, which he has observed in the course of his research. An annotated transcript for the edited TED Talk is on pages 77–79 of this Teacher's Guide.

TEACHING NOTES

The paragraph and questions introduce more ideas from Nic Marks. His theories about happiness, which students learned about in Lesson A, have led him to create the Happy Planet Index as an alternative to the GNP. Give students time to read the paragraph. Have students work individually to complete the activity. Point out that they should also use their background knowledge from Lesson A to help. Elicit a class discussion to check answers.

PART 1

PREVIEWING

A. Give students a couple of minutes to look over the graph. Explain that the infographic illustrates the Happy Planet Index. Tell students that Marks will explain it further in his TED Talk. Have students work individually to complete the activity.

B. Have students complete the activity in pairs. Have students check their answers to Exercises A and B as they watch the video during **Identifying Key Details**.

IDENTIFYING KEY DETAILS

A. Play the video. Tell students to check their answers to **Previewing** first. Then have students work individually to complete the sentences. Have them compare their answers in pairs. If necessary, play Part 1 again for students to check their answers. *Extension:* Ask students to work in pairs to paraphrase the summary paragraph.

RECOGNIZING A SPEAKER'S MESSAGE

A. Have students work individually to complete the activity before checking answers as a class. Note that in his talk, Marks first explains the Happy Planet Index and then talks more about why it's important for countries and societies to inform people more about these issues. Marks believes informing people will increase their motivation to improve both their ecological footprint and well-being on a personal and national level.

B. Give students a few minutes to think of examples of each. Then have them discuss and brainstorm their ideas in pairs before eliciting a class discussion. Write a concept map or a Venn diagram on the board of students' ideas. *Extension:* Ask students to go online and look up the most recent HPI and check their home countries. Do they think it's accurate? Why or why not?

CRITICAL THINKING

Questioning. Give students a few minutes to discuss their ideas with a partner. Critics of the HPI say it relies too much on ecological footprint and therefore champions poorer countries. And some argue that the survey of well-being is not accurate enough. For example, in some countries there is a vast difference in the everyday lives of men versus women. *Extension:* Have students go online to read some criticisms of the HPI.

PART 2

PREVIEWING

Give students a minute to think individually before sharing ideas in pairs. Tell them to write a list of five points they think are actions that will lead to happiness. If necessary, point out that they can use the background information that they learned in

1–3. Answers will vary. Possibilities include: **1.** Life expectancy can be measured by taking the average lifespan of a country's residents. Personal well-being can perhaps be measured via a survey of the general population. Ecological footprint can be measured by looking at a country's energy use and renewable resources.; **2.** Governments can focus on ecological footprint by using more renewable energy sources. The well-being of the people of a nation can be improved by access to good health care and good education, for example.

PART 1

Previewing

A. 1. happy life years; **2.** ecological footprint; **3.** Middle East; **4.** South Asia; **5.** Latin America

B. Guesses will vary. Actual answer is: Country 1 is Costa Rica.

Identifying Key Details

1. Costa Rica; **2.** 78; **3.** a quarter; **4.** 99; **5.** Army; **6.** literacy; **7.** social

Recognizing a Speaker's Message

A. The following should be underlined: government level, business level, personal level.

B. Answers will vary.

Critical Thinking

Questioning. Answers will vary.

PART 2

Previewing

Guesses will vary. Actual answers are: build social relationships, stay physically active, be aware of life around you, keep learning, give to others.

Recognizing Main Ideas and Examples

A. 1. Main Point: Connect; **Example:** Invest time and energy in loved ones, build relationships
2. Main Point: Be active; **Example:** Step outside, go for a walk, dance
3. Main Point: Take notice/Be mindful; **Example:** Be aware of seasons changing and people around you
4. Main Point: Keep learning; **Example:** Cook a new dish, learn to play an instrument
5. Main Point: Give; **Example:** Give to others, donate money

B. Answers will vary.

Critical Thinking

Applying. Answers will vary.

Lesson A. Elicit a class discussion to hear students' ideas. *Extension:* Take a poll to reach a consensus on the five actions the class thinks Marks is going to talk about. Write them on the board and ask students to give reasons or examples for each.

RECOGNIZING MAIN IDEAS AND EXAMPLES

A. Have students look over the chart first. Then play the video. If necessary, play the video twice so students can listen for both the main points and examples. Have students check their answers in pairs.

B. Give students five minutes to brainstorm additional examples for each point. Then have pairs share one new example for each point with the class. *Extension:* Ask students to work individually to rank how important each point is in their daily lives. Have them use this list in the **Critical Thinking** activity next.

CRITICAL THINKING

Applying. Give students a couple of minutes to think about Marks's points in relation to their own lives. Tell students to think about which points are part of their lives and which are lacking. Then have them share their ideas with a partner. *Extension:* Have students write letters to themselves to outline what they aspire to change over the next year in order to be happier.

EXPLORE MORE

Students can also go to happyplanetindex.org to learn more about Marks's HPI.

DESIGNING A PLAN FOR COMMUNITY HAPPINESS

PROJECT OVERVIEW

Aims:

- Students create a plan to raise the happiness level of their community.
- Students synthesize what they learned in the unit about well-being and happiness.
- Students present their plans, listen to others, and discuss them in detail.

Summary: Students write a plan for a project that aims to increase the HPI of their local communities. Students make a presentation about the plan, including how to fund it and its benefits, to two other pairs. Groups then discuss in detail each of the plans.

Materials: poster board, pens, tape, scissors, or computer and presentation software

Language Support: Talking about problems: *There is too much/are too many . . . ; There isn't/aren't enough . . .*
Talking about solutions: *This can help . . . ; This would improve . . . ; This would positively affect . . .*

TEACHING NOTES

PREPARATION

Have students work in pairs to think about the two main elements of their plan: what would make the community happier and what would have a positive environmental impact. Give them five minutes to brainstorm ideas and do research online if necessary. Then ask them to write an outline of their plan. Check each outline to make sure it contains useful ideas. If not, help steer pairs by asking them questions about their plans to get them thinking more. Remind them to also consider how they will find funding. Note the "Language Support" phrases above on the board and review them before students begin the activity.

DURING THE PROJECT

Tell pairs to be prepared to talk about the positive outcome that their plans aim to create, and how this will increase the HPI of the community. If students make posters, give them time to draw pictures and add information about their plan. Monitor as students work together to create their presentations. Then have pairs present to each other.

AFTER THE PROJECT

Have each group discuss the plans presented in detail. Tell them to ask each other if the plans are realistic, if they are doable and cost-effective, as well as if they would really raise the HPI of the community. Tell students to use the questions on page 71 to guide their discussions. If necessary, write the questions on the board for students to refer to as they discuss. Encourage group members to give suggestions on how to make each plan better. ***Extension:*** Have each group choose which plan they think is the best and present it to the class.

CAREER PATHS

UNIT OVERVIEW

Reading: Students read about one man's experience of taking a year off from his job.

TED Talk: Graphic designer Stefan Sagmeister talks about how taking a sabbatical every seven years has positively affected his career and his life.

Project: Students design a plan for employees to get work leave.

 ## MY YEAR IN THE ARCTIC

LESSON OVERVIEW

Aims:
- Read and comprehend an essay about one family's year off on a remote Nordic island.
- Understand sequence and reasons.
- Understand figurative language.

Target Vocabulary: couple, ethics, hesitate, income, mentally, physically, reliable, reserved

Reading Passage Summary: Students read a personal essay written by an American man who decided to take a year off from work and move with his family to a remote part of the world.

TEACHING NOTES

THINK AND DISCUSS

This unit looks at the power and effect of taking time off from your work and career. Ask students to look at the picture and think about their own dreams about travel and hopes for their life experiences. Then ask them if they think it's possible to accomplish these while having a full-time career. Can students imagine taking a year off in the middle of their working life? Have students discuss their answers in pairs. Then elicit students' ideas and opinions, encouraging them to give reasons and examples to support them. *Extension:* Ask students to share what work schedules are typically like in their home countries.

PRE-READING

A. Give students one minute to read the caption and the paragraph on page 74 introducing the reading passage. Then give them a few minutes to think about pros and cons and write their answers. Have them share their answers with a partner, brainstorming some additional ideas together. Elicit students' ideas, writing them on the board. *Extension:* Take a class poll to see how many students think Chen's idea is smart or not. Ask students to support their opinions with reasons. At the end of the unit, take the poll again to see if students' opinions have changed.

B. Have students read the questions first before scanning for information. Make sure students understand that scanning involves looking quickly for

Think and Discuss

1. and 2. Answers will vary.

Pre-reading

A. Answers will vary. Possibilities include: **Pros:** a break from work, more time with family, an adventurous life change; **Cons:** challenging new life, hard to move a whole family, no friends or relatives, hard to find work again after a year off

B. 1. They moved to Rødøy, Norway, in the Arctic.; **2.** They were inspired by a TED Talk by Stefan Sagmeister.

C. The experience was positive. Chen says it was life-changing, and gave him new confidence for and a fresh perspective on both his work and personal life.

Getting the Main Ideas

The following should be checked: 1, 3, 4, 5.

Understanding Sequence

A. a. 5; **b.** 8; **c.** 1; **d.** 7; **e.** 4; **f.** 2; **g.** 6; **h.** 3

B. Answers may vary. Possibilities include: 3, 4, 5, 6, 9.

Understanding Reasons

Reasons should appear in the following order: f, e, a, c, b.

Understanding Figurative Language

A. 1. e; **2.** d; **3.** c; **4.** a; **5.** g; **6.** b; **7.** f

B. 1. something that is burned to create power, such as gasoline in an engine; **2.** verb; **3.** give it new energy

Building Vocabulary

A. 1. ethic; **2.** hesitate; **3.** mentally; **4.** physical; **5.** enrich

B. 1. c; **2.** d; **3.** a; **4.** e; **5.** b

Getting Meaning from Context

A. 1. e; **2.** b; **3.** g; **4.** a; **5.** f; **6.** c; **7.** d

B. Answers will vary.

Critical Thinking

1. Evaluating. Answers will vary. Some possible challenges include: finding a new job, adjusting to regular life.
2. Interpreting. Chen explains that they were less anxious and more at peace with themselves and their lives.

Explore More

Chen talks about how coming back to the U.S. with the knowledge that he and his family could live on very little on a remote island gave him the confidence to develop and sell his app.

specific information. Have them work individually to complete the activity. Give them 30 seconds to complete it before checking answers in pairs.

C. Point out that students should read the last paragraph, not scan or skim. Have them work individually to answer the questions before checking answers as a class. Ask students to support their ideas with evidence from the paragraph. *Extension:* Point out that Chen says in the last paragraph that he discovered a new kind of work as a result of his year off. Ask students to guess what kind of work. Have them check their guesses as they read. Possible answer include: programming and software development.

DEVELOPING READING SKILLS

GETTING THE MAIN IDEAS

Have students read the entire passage, either silently or while listening to the narrated passage on the audio.

Have them work individually to complete the activity before checking answers in pairs. *Extension:* Ask pairs to work together to organize the summary statements and then paraphrase them.

UNDERSTANDING SEQUENCE

A. Give students a couple of minutes to read the sentences. Have them work individually to put them in the correct sequence before checking answers as a class. Elicit the events one by one, writing a timeline on the board as students say the answers. *Extension:* Encourage a discussion about how listening to a TED Talk changed Winston Chen's life. By this point in the textbook, students have listened to a number of TED Talks. Ask them if any have inspired them to make changes, big or small. Have students share with a partner.

B. Have students work in pairs to complete the activity. Note that answers may vary depending how students interpret each step. For example, while Chen found inspiration from Sagmeister to take the big step of taking a year off, he did not find inspiration from anyone in deciding how to spend his time. He decided his plan was to have a year without goals.

UNDERSTANDING REASONS

Explain that the events in the chart are the results. Tell students to match each reason with the result. Have students work individually to complete the activity before checking answers as a class. *Extension:* Point out for item **a.** that Chen's decision to leave might have been very different if he had not been bored with his job at the time he heard the TED Talk. Ask students to find other results that might have changed if Chen's situation or attitude at the time had been different.

UNDERSTANDING FIGURATIVE LANGUAGE

A. Explain that figurative language goes beyond its literal meaning and is quite common in writing, especially literary writing. Chen's writing style employs a lot of figurative language. Tell students to study the context to guess the meaning of an unknown term by looking at the words around it, and how it is used in the sentence. Have students work in pairs to complete the activity before checking answers as a class. *Extension:* Have students work in pairs to look at both the literal definition and the figurative meaning of each term. Tell them to share if they have any terms with similar figurative meanings in their native languages. Ask them to explain the term to their partners.

B. Have students work individually to answer the questions. Tell students to make educated guesses if they are not sure what "fuel your career" means. Check answers together as a class. *Extension:* Have students each write a sentence containing the verb *fuel*. Ask for volunteers to read theirs to the class. Have the class check whether it is a correct use of the verb or not.

BUILDING VOCABULARY

A. Have students work individually to complete the sentences before checking answers in pairs. The term *work ethic* refers to a person's sense of commitment to work. If you have a good *work ethic*, you are considered a hard worker. An *ethic* is a moral principle that dictates the way someone acts. When a person acts honestly or morally, his or her behavior is *ethical*.

B. Have students work individually before checking answers in pairs. When *reserve* is used as a verb, it means to save something to use later. As an adjective, *reserved* can mean to save something, such as a reserved table at a restaurant. An unrelated use of *reserved* can describe the behavior of someone who is reluctant to be too emotional: *My grandmother is a bit reserved.*

GETTING MEANING FROM CONTEXT

A. Have students work individually to complete the activity. Encourage them to go back to the reading passage to look at the phrases being used in context. Check answers as a class. *Extension:* Have students write new sentences using the phrases in the activity.

B. Have students work in pairs. Elicit or explain the meaning of "going through the motions." Make sure students understand that it is generally used in a negative way because you're mentally or emotionally disconnected from whatever action you're doing. For example, *After his wife died, he lost his will to live; he's just going through the motions.* Give students a few minutes to discuss with partners. If time permits, elicit some examples that students discussed.

CRITICAL THINKING

1. Evaluating. Give students time to go back to their pro and con lists. Have them discuss in pairs first before eliciting a class discussion. If the pro and con list is still on the board, refer to this for the class discussion. Ask students to comment on any pros or cons that Chen talked about that surprised them. *Extension:* Ask students to think again about whether they think it's a smart idea to take a year off. Have their ideas changed after reading the passage? Would they want to do it themselves?

2. Interpreting. Have students share their ideas in pairs. Remind students of the discussion they had in question 3 of **Pre-reading**. Elicit a class discussion about how Chen's year off changed him and his family. *Extension:* To add to the class discussion, ask students to share any personal experiences they've had with taking time off or taking a meaningful vacation and how it changed them.

EXPLORE MORE

Chen also has a personal blog that documents his entire year in the Arctic: arcticdream.me.

THE POWER OF TIME OFF

LESSON OVERVIEW

Aims:
- Watch and understand a talk about the benefits of taking time off from work.
- Understand main ideas and key details.
- Understand causes and effects.

TED Talk Summary: In his TED Talk, graphic designer Stefan Sagmeister shares how taking a one-year sabbatical every seven years has transformed him and his design business, both for the better. Sagmeister closes his company for one year every seven years, giving himself and his employees time off to pursue creative and personal interests. He talks in detail about how he's learned to use this year off to make it worthwhile and shows us how ideas he's gotten while taking time off have affected his work as a designer. Note that Sagmeister is the TED speaker who inspired Lesson A writer Winston Chen. An annotated transcript for the edited TED Talk is on pages 80–82 of this Teacher's Guide.

TEACHING NOTES

The paragraph and questions introduce Sagmeister's work and career. Have students read the paragraph individually before writing their answers. Then have them check answers in pairs. For question 2, encourage students to go back to Unit 4 to review Nic Marks's Happy Planet Index and the five keys to happiness that he shares. Check answers by having students draw a Venn diagram of the two speakers' ideas on the board. Note that in addition to being a TED speaker four times, Sagmeister is also the author of numerous books, including *Things I Have Learned in My Life So Far*. **Extension:** Have students work in pairs to go online and find some examples of Sagmeister's design work.

PART 1

PREVIEWING

A. Have students complete Exercise A in pairs. Tell them to brainstorm a list of ideas that they think they'll hear based on what they read in Lesson A. Then have pairs share one or two ideas with the class. Write a mind map on the board of their ideas.

B. Give students a minute to go back and read the quote from Sagmeister. Have them work individually to answer the questions. Play the video for students to check their answers.

UNDERSTANDING MAIN IDEAS

Have students work individually to answer the question before discussing their answers in pairs. Ask students to think about Chen's story as well. Did the two men have similar reasons for taking time off? Point out that in Sagmeister's case, he actually closes his entire business for the year. Ask students to discuss the difference between that and Chen leaving his job.

Extension: Ask students to work in pairs to paraphrase the following line from Sagmeister's talk: "But probably even more important is that the work that comes out of these years flows back into the company and into society at large, rather than just benefiting a grandchild or two."

UNDERSTANDING KEY DETAILS

A. Have students work individually to complete the activity before checking answers in pairs. **Extension:** Have students work in pairs to read a summary of Haidt's talk online at TED.com, or have them watch the talk.

B. Have students work in pairs to complete the activity. Check answers as a class, eliciting explanations of *job, career,* and *calling* in students' own words. **Extension:** Have students write a one-page essay about their work life or their future work life and what they hope each level of it will be like.

CRITICAL THINKING

Synthesizing. Give students a few minutes to discuss their ideas with a partner. Then elicit a class discussion. Ask students to support their ideas with examples from Chen's essay. **Extension:** To encourage further class discussion, ask students to think about people they know who are working (or themselves if they have jobs) and to describe that person's work life using Haidt's three levels of work.

1. graphic design; 2. Sagmeister thinks our relationships with others matter most. Marks agrees that social connections are important, but he also thinks happiness is connected to well-being and ecological footprint. Social connection is only one of Marks's five keys to happiness.

PART 1

Previewing

A. Answers will vary. Students should infer that the talk discusses the benefits of taking a year off.

B. He decided to use five of his retirement years now, one every seven years, and extend his working years as he ages instead.

Understanding Main Ideas

He found that he was getting bored with his job and that the quality and originality of his work were both suffering.

Understanding Key Details

A. The following should be underlined: job, career, calling.

B. a. calling; **b.** job; **c.** career

Critical Thinking

Synthesizing. A job. When he came back, he had found his calling.

PART 2

Predicting

1. and 2. Answers will vary.

Understanding Causes and Effects

A. 1. He wrote a detailed plan and schedule.; **2.** The approach was successful and helped him become a better designer as well. When he went back to work, he was able to increase his fees as a result.

Understanding Key Details

1. c, e; **2.** d, f; **3.** a, b

Critical Thinking

1. Evaluating. Answers will vary. Time off from work gives people the freedom to work on more personal projects, which they can later bring back to their companies and careers.
2. Personalizing. Answers will vary.

PART 2

PREDICTING

Have students work individually to read the excerpt and think about their answers to the questions. Make sure students read the definitions in the footnotes to help them understand the excerpt. Give them a minute to think of their answers before having them discuss in pairs. Note that Chen and Sagmeister approached the planning of their sabbaticals differently. Ask students to think about what they would do and why. Play the video to have them check their answers. *Extension:* Ask students who said they would make a specific plan to share some ideas for it with their partners.

UNDERSTANDING CAUSES AND EFFECTS

Have students work individually to read the excerpt and answer the questions. Note that students can also use the excerpt in **Predicting** to help them answer the questions as they are comparing his first and second approaches to the sabbatical. Make sure students understand that the cause of his change in approach was his lack of initial success. He explains he was not making good use of his time off until he made a very organized plan. Point out that this is different from Chen's approach. If necessary, play the video again to have students check their answers. *Extension:* Elicit additional causes and effects that Sagmeister mentions in his talk.

UNDERSTANDING KEY DETAILS

Have students look at the location and details of Sagmeister's projects. Elicit an explanation about when these projects happened. Make sure students understand that these projects each happened after his sabbatical, by which they should infer that the inspiration for these projects came about during the time when his company was closed. *Extension:* Elicit a class discussion about the projects. What do students think about them? How do these projects compare to the ones Sagmeister created before the company sabbatical?

CRITICAL THINKING

1. Evaluating. If necessary, play Part 2 of the video again so students can hear the names of the companies he talks about one more time. Or elicit the company names and a brief explanation of what each is known for. Have students work individually at first to think of disadvantages and advantages. Point out that this is the same as pros and cons. Have students compare and discuss their lists with a partner or the class.

2. Personalizing. Give students five minutes to think about and write a plan for their sabbatical. Tell them to also write notes about how they will prepare for it. Then have students share their plans with a group. Ask group members to support each other by making suggestions about how to make their plans even better.

EXPLORE MORE

Note that Sagmeister has given three other TED Talks. Encourage students to see what else he has to say.

CREATING A TIME-OFF PLAN FOR EMPLOYEES

PROJECT OVERVIEW

Aims:
- Students create a time-off program for employees of their companies.
- Students synthesize what they learned in the unit and use it to create their plans.
- Students present their plans and take a vote to decide which one is best.

Summary: Students create a time-off program and present it to other pairs. Groups discuss pros and cons of each plan and vote on their favorite.

Materials: computer, presentation software and/or poster board, pens

Language Support: Discussing: *What do you think about . . . ? What are your thoughts on . . . ?*

TEACHING NOTES

PREPARATION

Have students work in pairs. Explain that they are co-owners of a company with employees, and they want to create a time-off program that everyone can benefit from. Tell students to use what they learned in the unit to support their ideas. Ask students to first decide what kind of company they have and what kinds of jobs their employees have. Point out that students will have to explain this background information in their presentations. Note the "Language Support" phrases on the board and review them before students begin the activity.

DURING THE PROJECT

Tell students to use the questions on page 87 to guide their process as they create their plans. Remind them to think about the kind of employees they have, the kind of company they have, and the benefits they want both to experience as a result of the time-off program. Monitor as pairs work on their plans together. Point out that students only have two minutes for their presentations, so they should think about the most efficient way to present their ideas. Give students five to ten minutes to create their program plans. Then give them a few minutes to practice their presentations before presenting to two other pairs.

AFTER THE PROJECT

As pairs present, tell the listeners to take notes. Remind them to think about pros and cons for each program. Give students time to review their notes and then ask groups to discuss each other's programs. Encourage members to make suggestions for improving each other's programs. After pairs are finished discussing, ask them to choose one plan to present to the class. After each group has presented, have the class vote on the best time-off program. Ask students to give reasons and examples to explain their votes. *Extension:* Tell students that they are employees of the winning company. Ask them to share with their groups what they plan to do during their time off.

TEXT GENERATION

UNIT OVERVIEW

Reading: Students read about the difference between spoken and written language and where texting fits in.

TED Talk: Linguist John McWhorter explains how texting is actually an exciting new form of communication.

Project: Students analyze a text conversation and present about its terms and their meaning.

 **Lesson 6A** THE DEATH OF WRITING?

LESSON OVERVIEW

Aims:
- Read and comprehend an article that analyzes how texting is expanding language.
- Make comparisons.
- Understand contrastive language.

Target Vocabulary: conscious, decline, edit, expand on, feedback, formal, linguist, logically, mode, spontaneous

Reading Passage Summary: Students read about how texting is changing language. The abbreviations that are a common part of texting are not used in any other form of written language—which is one change. Linguist John McWhorter argues, though, that texting isn't a form of written language at all; instead, it is something new altogether. With texting, people are writing like they speak, which means their language choice is more spontaneous and less reflective. Instead of being a sign of linguistic decline, McWhorter insists texting is instead a new form of discourse, which is expanding our communication.

TEACHING NOTES

THINK AND DISCUSS

Have students work individually to write a list of all the ways they've communicated with family and friends over the last three days. Then have them compare in pairs and talk about their preferred modes of communication and why they like them. Ask them to think about which people they use different modes of communication for, such as parents versus friends. For question 2, ask students to count how many texts they've sent in the last 24 hours. Then take a poll and write the results on the board. Ask students to calculate the class's daily texting average. Elicit examples of when and why students text.

PRE-READING

A. Give students a few minutes to work individually to read the title and introduction, and write their answers. Elicit a class discussion to hear students' thoughts on the topic. **_Extension:_** Before students read the passage, have them write an opinion essay about what

Think and Discuss

1. Answers will vary. Possibilities include: face-to-face, by phone, by texts; by email, by video calls, etc.;
2. Answers will vary.

Pre-reading

A. 1. Since texting doesn't follow the rules of grammar or spelling, some feel that it's killing writing as we know it.

B. 1. and 2. Answers will vary.

C. Answers will vary.

Getting the Main Ideas

The following should be checked: 1, 3, 4, 5.

Understanding Key Details

1. 76,800/77,000; **2.** 3,600; **3.** hour; **4.** writing

Making Comparisons

A. a. s; **b.** s; **c.** w; **d.** w

B. Answers will vary. Possibilities from the passage include:
Speaking: primary, fundamental mode of communication; everyone learns to speak; telegraphic, spontaneous, less reflective; formal speech is more like writing

Writing: not everyone learns it; allows for deep thinking, evaluation, and editing of ideas; texting is written communication that is more like speaking

Understanding Contrastive Language

A. The following statements should be underlined:
Paragraph 3: McWhorter points out that . . .
Paragraph 4: And while just about everyone . . .
Paragraph 7: While they are different forms . . .
Sidebar: While concerns about linguistic . . .

B. Paragraph 3: a; Paragraph 4: b; Paragraph 7: b; Sidebar: a

Building Vocabulary

A. 1. formal; **2.** mode; **3.** spontaneous; **4.** edit; **5.** conscious

B. 1. b; **2.** a; **3.** b; **4.** b; **5.** a

Getting Meaning from Context

1. a; **2.** a; **3.** a

Critical Thinking

Interpreting. McWhorter calls texting a new form of communication and says it is broadening our language use and interaction with language rather than limiting it.

---

categories they think texting fits into linguistically and how texting may be affecting language. After students have completed the unit, have them revisit their essays and see if their opinions have changed.

B. Point out that students should only read the headings in the passage, not skim the content. Ask them to share their own ideas about language and speaking and writing. Encourage students to support their ideas with reasons and examples. After pairs discuss, elicit a class discussion to hear students' ideas. Make a Venn diagram for speaking and writing on the board for question 2. Encourage students to think about both differences and similarities.

C. Have students work in pairs to look at the infographic and discuss which abbreviations they know. Tell students to comment on which ones they like and which ones they use often. Ask students to add any additional ones that they know to the list. Elicit these and their meanings. Write them on the board.

DEVELOPING READING SKILLS

GETTING THE MAIN IDEAS

Have students read the entire passage, either silently or while listening to the narrated passage on the audio. Have them work individually to check the statements for Exercise A before checking answers in pairs. Point out or elicit the role of the two statements that are not main ideas; each is a key detail or supporting idea.

UNDERSTANDING KEY DETAILS

Have students work individually to complete the activity. Note that some of the answers are paraphrases of the information in the passage, instead of verbatim. For question 1, the adjective *about* in the sentences means that students may have a slight range of answers. The exact number based on the data in the passage is 76,800 years ago, but students may round this to 77,000.

MAKING COMPARISONS

A. Give students two minutes to work individually to complete the activity before checking answers in pairs. Elicit the answers, writing them in a chart on the board to build on in Exercise B.

B. Give students a few minutes to write ideas individually. Then have them share with a partner and brainstorm some more ideas together. Elicit ideas from each pair, writing them in the chart on the board. *Extension:* If not already discussed in the **Pre-reading**, make a Venn diagram instead of a chart and encourage students to not only come up with differences between writing and speaking, but similarities, too.

UNDERSTANDING CONTRASTIVE LANGUAGE

A. Explain that the conjunction *while* is one example of contrasting language. Elicit other phrases that do the same job: *although, whereas, in contrast, at the same time,* etc. Give students one minute to complete the activity. Note that the last statement is from the sidebar *The Decline of Language?* and not in the main passage. *Extension:* Have students work in pairs to make a list of more contrasting language. Possibilities include: *whereas, though, in contrast, but* etc.

B. Have students work individually to complete the activity before checking answers in pairs.

BUILDING VOCABULARY

A. Have students complete Exercise A individually before checking answers in pairs. The noun *mode* is a synonym for *way*. It refers to the manner in which something is experienced. The adjective *conscious* is used to show that someone is aware of what's being done. While it can also mean "awake," in the passage, *conscious* is used to talk about awareness. *Extension:* Ask students to work in pairs to summarize the paragraph.

B. Have students complete Exercise B individually before checking answers in pairs. The term *feedback* is used in many fields, especially business and academics, to talk about formal reactions from people such as co-workers or customers or teachers. However, we also use it to refer to comments and reactions from others to what we've said or written in more personal conversations. *Extension:* Ask students to each write a comment, or feedback, about the passage. What do they think about the ideas in it? The writing style? The overall message? If possible, have them write their comments as text messages.

GETTING MEANING FROM CONTEXT

Have students work individually to complete the activity before checking their answers in pairs. Note for question 3 that a synonym for *spells* is *leads to*. *Extension:* Have students rewrite the sentences in paragraph 1 using synonyms for each of the words in the activity.

CRITICAL THINKING

Interpreting. Have students discuss the questions in pairs before eliciting a class discussion for each. Encourage students to also discuss whether they agree with McWhorter or not. *Extension:* To encourage more discussion, ask students to think about their parents or grandparents. Will texting also expand their linguistic repertoire? Encourage a light debate about the older generation and this new style of communication.

EXPLORE MORE

Pagel is a biologist who suggests that language and social cooperation have always gone hand in hand. In fact, according to Pagel, this is how language first developed.

LESSON OVERVIEW

Aims:
- Watch and understand a talk about how texting is expanding our linguistic repertoire.
- Understand key details.
- Apply and summarize information.

TED Talk Summary: In his TED Talk, linguist John McWhorter analyzes texting from an academic standpoint, and talks about how it's changing language. While many think texting is a sign of the decline of language, McWhorter argues that in fact it is a sign of how language is broadening, expanding, and evolving. He argues that it's a new category of language, as it fits into neither speaking nor writing. He takes a look at some text conversations, and explains the context in which some new terms are being used. He also discusses the linguistic significance of this new form of communication being pioneered by young people. An annotated transcript for the edited TED Talk is on pages 83–84 of this Teacher's Guide.

TEACHING NOTES

Have students work individually to read the paragraph and answer the questions. Students have already been introduced to McWhorter and his ideas in Lesson A. The information on page 98 introduces his professional background and says more about his own personal texting habits. Note that the questions bring up an important topic in regard to texting: age. Ask students to share examples of the difference in texting styles between older and younger generations. **Extension:** Divide the class into groups of three and have students discuss how age affects texting. Challenge them to make their entire discussion in text messages. Have them write down their comments for the other two members to see and respond to. Encourage them to use the texting terms they learned in Lesson A.

PART 1

PREVIEWING

A. Have students complete Exercise A individually before checking answers as a class. Encourage students to expand on McWhorter's definition of "fingered speech." What does he mean? Can they put this term in their own words? For question 2, elicit or explain what McWhorter means by "bagginess of structure." Make sure students understand that he means that the structure of texting is loose and informal, not anything like what we are used to when we study language in the classroom. Note that question 3 points out that in fact texting is introducing a "new structure," a thought that connects back to one of the concerns mentioned in question 2. **Extension:** Have students work in small groups to brainstorm some ideas about what this new structure is. Then have them share their ideas with the class.

B. Play the video. Tell students to check their ideas as they watch.

UNDERSTANDING KEY DETAILS

Give students a few minutes to read the paragraph and complete the activity. Point out that the notes are a summary of the content in the paragraph. Check answers as a class. Elicit or explain the meaning of *empathy, accommodation,* and *pragmatic particles.* **Extension:** Ask students to share any pragmatic particles common in their native languages. Tell them to give an example of how the particle is used.

PART 2

PREDICTING

A. Give students a minute to work individually to read the conversation. Then have them discuss their ideas in pairs. Note that students' predictions may not be correct, but encourage them to analyze how the term is used in the conversation. Elicit their ideas.

B. Play the video. Tell students to check their ideas as they watch. After the video, elicit or explain the two uses of *slash* that McWhorter talks about. **Extension:** Ask students to explain the meaning of Jake's last text. McWhorter explains that he isn't even sure what Jake is saying after "slash." Have students work in pairs to try to guess the meaning. (Jake is probably watching an online video of basketball players trying to shoot baskets with one eye closed.)

APPLYING INFORMATION

A. Explain that students are now going to try to do what McWhorter does: analyze language. Point out

1. He is a linguist who focuses on how language has evolved and will continue to evolve due to social, historical, and technological forces.; **2.** He says that his age, 46, makes him too old to be fluent at texting since it is primarily a language used by young people.; **3.** Answers will vary. Students should recognize that in many ways, texting is a written form of speaking.

PART 1

Previewing

A. 1. The following should be underlined: fingered speech.; **2.** bagginess of the structure, the lack of concern with rules; **3.** Texting is a new type of language that follows its own structure instead of the rules learned in school.

Understanding Key Details

1. empathy; **2.** pragmatic particle; **3.** ne; **4.** yo

PART 2

Predicting

A. Predictions will vary. The word *slash* is used to change the topic.

Applying Information

A. 1. c; **2.** b; **3.** d; **4.** a

B. Answers will vary.

Summarizing Information

The following should be checked: 1st, 2nd, 4th, and 5th sentences.

Critical Thinking

1. Evaluating. Answers will vary.

2. Personalizing. Answers will vary.

---

that the conversations in the activity are not from McWhorter's talk, but each underlined term is a language marker common in speaking (not writing). Students may already be familiar with some of the terms. Give them a few minutes to work individually to complete the activity before checking answers in pairs. *Extension:* Ask pairs to write a new conversation using each language marker.

B. Have students work in pairs first to discuss language markers in other languages that they know. Ask them to use examples to explain the markers' use and purpose. Then have pairs share with the class.

SUMMARIZING INFORMATION

Give students two minutes to work individually to complete the activity. Check answers as a class, eliciting students' thoughts and opinions about each point. If students are in the right age range, ask them how they feel about being part of creating a brand-new language. If they are not in that age range, ask them how they feel about what McWhorter is saying. *Extension:* Encourage further discussion by asking students to comment on what texting is like in their home countries and native languages. Do McWhorter's ideas apply?

CRITICAL THINKING

1. Evaluating. Give students time to think about their answer to the question. Ask them to consider how McWhorter's argument could be stronger, such as he could offer more examples of conversations and new language markers. Tell students to also think about what they wish had been in McWhorter's talk that wasn't. One example might be a discussion about whether this new language is going to create a problematic generation gap or not. *Extension:* Encourage further conversation by asking students to think about how texting may evolve further as the texting generation ages and their lifestyles and responsibilities change. Will they still be texting *lol* and *haha* when they are the same age as McWhorter?

2. Personalizing. Have students share with a partner any personal stories of miscommunications they've had while texting. Ask for volunteers to tell their stories with the class. Have the class discuss how each miscommunication could have been avoided.

EXPLORE MORE

If students haven't already discussed this topic, tell them to think about how texting is going to change as the young generation who started it gets older. Encourage students to also discuss other ways that language is changing in modern times.

PRESENTING AN ANALYSIS OF HOW PEOPLE USE TEXTING

PROJECT OVERVIEW

Aims:
- Students collect and analyze some text conversations.
- Students present on what they learned about how and why people text.

Summary: Students look closely at some examples of text conversations. They analyze the meanings of the conversations. Then pairs present to others about their analyses. Groups discuss the texts from each presentation and say how they support McWhorter's ideas or not.

Materials: computer/smartphone, Internet, poster board or paper or presentation software

Language Support: To show amazement: *Really?; Wow, . . . ; How interesting.*

TEACHING NOTES

PREPARATION

Have students work in pairs. Explain that students should try to use examples of a conversation instead of just one text. Ask them to use texts from their own phones or to make up text conversations or find some examples online. Note the "Language Support" phrases above on the board and review them before students begin the activity.

DURING THE PROJECT

Give pairs enough time to analyze the meaning of each conversation. Tell them to focus especially on new terms and language markers. Ask them to use the questions on page 103 as a guide for their analysis. Remind students that they saw McWhorter do a similar analysis in his TED Talk. Tell them to use his as a model for their presentation style. Monitor as pairs work on their analyses together. If necessary, help them with understanding the language and context in the texts. (Make sure students don't use texts with any inappropriate content.) Give students a few minutes to practice their presentations. Then divide the class into groups of three pairs for presentations and discussion.

AFTER THE PROJECT

After each pair presents for two minutes, tell groups to discuss what they heard and learned. Tell them to talk about which new terms they like the most, and which are the easiest to use. Ask them to discuss if the language in the presentation supports McWhorter's ideas or not. Have a class discussion to elicit new terms, along with their meaning and use, from each group. Write the terms on the board. **Extension:** Have pairs work with another pair. Ask them to have a conversation via text. Tell one pair to write the first line on a piece of paper, then pass it to the other pair who writes a response, and so on. Encourage students to use the new terms they've learned.

EXPLORE MORE

Curzan shares interesting and funny anecdotes about new words and dictionaries, and how language is forever evolving.

BARRIERS AND BRIDGES

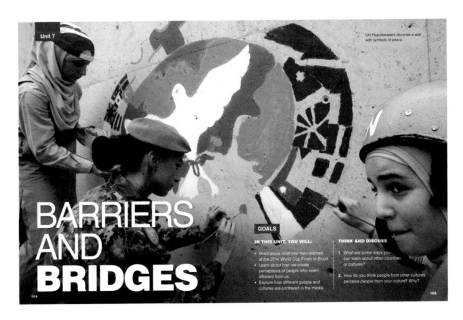

UNIT OVERVIEW

Reading: Students read about how one man experienced global relations first hand during an international sporting event.

TED Talk: Writer Chimamanda Ngozi Adichie talks about the danger of having a one-dimensional image of a people or country.

Project: Students analyze a fictitious character and decide if the portrayal is encouraging a stereotype or not.

 ## BRINGING THE WORLD TOGETHER

LESSON OVERVIEW

Aims:
- Read and comprehend a personal essay about experiencing camaraderie and connection between cultures during the 2014 World Cup.
- Understand the author's tone and purpose.

Target Vocabulary: apologizing, attending, break up, broke out, coincides, diversity, ignored, isolated, opponents, potential

Reading Passage Summary: Students read an essay adapted from a blog post about a Palestinian man's experience of cultural bonding during the 2014 World Cup in Brazil. Aziz Abu Sarah talks about how soccer fans are often portrayed as aggressive and even violent toward each other, yet he experienced the exact opposite during the World Cup. He saw fans from opposing teams help break up fights, comfort each other, and even apologize when one team beat the other. He writes about soccer as a uniting force between cultures and countries, one that gives the people of the world the opportunity to get to know each other better.

TEACHING NOTES

THINK AND DISCUSS

This unit focuses on how we learn about and perceive other cultures. It asks students to take a look at how portrayals of other cultures and people in the media and literature affect our impressions and views of each other, and how, in fact, real interaction with people of different nations gives us a more accurate and compassionate understanding of each other. Use question 1 to elicit ways in which we are presented images of other cultures, such as in the media or in stories, as well as ways in which we experience other cultures on a personal level. For question 2, ask students to share stereotypes about people from their home countries as well as opinions or stories that show alternate images as well.

Think and Discuss

1. Answers will vary. Possibilities include: from individuals directly, by visiting other countries, by watching TV or movies, by reading stories or articles, by tasting cuisines, etc.; **2.** Answers will vary.

Pre-reading

A. 1–3. Answers will vary.

B. Guesses will vary. Actual answer is that the writer learned that people of varying nations are more supportive of and kind to each other than the media typically portrays.

Getting the Main Ideas

1. He remembered as a young boy watching the World Cup finals with his family on their brand-new television.; **2.** b; **3.** He believes that people get the chance to learn about other countries and cultures through soccer tournaments like the World Cup.

Understanding the Author's Tone and Purpose

A. A Childhood Dream: d; **Friends and Strangers:** a; **Building Bridges:** b

B. Answers may vary. Possibilities include:

A Childhood Dream: memory of watching finals with family; soccer was his favorite sport

Friends and Strangers: fans on both sides tried to end, not encourage, a fight that broke out; German fans comforted Brazilians in a bar when Brazil lost to Germany

Building Bridges: the world learned from Muslim players about Ramadan and fasting; soccer unites people

C. Details will vary. Possibilities include:

sentimental: attending the World Cup has been a dream since childhood

inspired: struck by camaraderie and friendships at games, found it spirit-lifting

joyful: happy to be surrounded by the excited buzz of other fans

optimistic: believes sports is ultimately a force for uniting people

D. c

Building Vocabulary

A. 1. attending; **2.** opponent; **3.** apologized; **4.** diversity; **5.** potential

B. 1. c; **2.** a; **3.** a; **4.** d; **5.** c

Getting Meaning from Context

A. 1. e; **2.** c; **3.** a; **4.** g; **5.** b; **6.** f; **7.** h; **8.** d

B. Answers will vary. Possibilities include: music festivals, celebrations like Mardi Gras, parties, food festivals, natural disasters or other large tragedies

Critical Thinking

Evaluating. Answers will vary.

PRE-READING

A. Give students a few minutes to work individually to answer the questions. Tell them to think about any event that they've been to where people from different countries have come together. Have students share their answers in pairs. Encourage them to share any anecdotes or examples to support their ideas. *Extension:* Have students write a blog to describe the experience.

B. Have students work in pairs. Give them one minute to look at the headings and discuss together before writing their answers. Elicit predictions. Students should infer that the essay is about an experience of bonding between people of different countries. From the pictures and the **Think and Discuss,** they can probably guess the author is writing about soccer.

DEVELOPING READING SKILLS

GETTING THE MAIN IDEAS

Have students read the entire passage, either silently or while listening to the narrated passage on the audio. Have them work individually to complete the activity before checking answers in pairs.

UNDERSTANDING THE AUTHOR'S TONE AND PURPOSE

A. Have students work individually to complete the activity. Check answers with Exercise B.

B. Give students a few minutes to go back to the passage to get details for the concept map. Review examples of support: stories, quotes, and statistics.

Note that students may pick up different details, or paraphrase them differently. Check answers as a class, pointing out that answers may vary slightly.

C. Explain that students should first think about the author's overall tone and choose the three attitudes from the list that are closest to this. If students need help, first elicit whether his overall tone is positive, negative, or neutral. Then tell them to choose attitudes and find support from there. Note that there are four possible options for tone. Point out that *sentimental* is generally considered a positive feeling of nostalgia, such as what the author describes in his childhood memories of watching the World Cup and playing soccer.

D. Have students work individually to answer the question before checking answers as a class. Elicit further explanation of the writer's main purpose. How can the World Cup accomplish this?

BUILDING VOCABULARY

A. Have students complete Exercise A individually before checking answers as a class. The word *diversity* is one of the key themes of the unit. Point out that diversity can refer not just to people but also to thoughts, opinions, experiences, etc.

B. Have students complete Exercise B individually before checking answers as a class. Point out that *broke out* and *break up* are both phrasal verbs. Another common use of the term *break up* is to describe the end of a romantic relationship. Elicit other phrasal verbs with *break* and their meanings: *break through, break in, break down, break off,* etc. *Extension:* Have students work individually to write sentences for each vocabulary word in the activity.

GETTING MEANING FROM CONTEXT

A. Have students work individually or in pairs to complete Exercises A and B before checking answers as a class. Elicit example sentences for each word when checking answers. *Extension:* Have students search for example sentences online to see the terms in use. Ask them to explain the meaning of the sentence to a partner.

B. Have students work in pairs or small groups to discuss the questions. Encourage them to brainstorm a list of possible events or situations that bring people together. Then elicit examples from each pair or group. *Extension:* Ask each student to explain to a partner which kind of event, from the ones discussed, they'd most like to go to and why.

CRITICAL THINKING

Evaluating. Give students a few minutes to think about and write their answers before sharing with a partner. Abu Sarah's point is that the media tends to focus on negative experiences and encounters, whereas the reality is that the majority of experiences and encounters being had between people of different countries are positive. *Extension:* Ask students to also consider and discuss why the media tends to focus on the negative.

EXPLORE MORE

Abu Sarah's talk is less than five minutes, which may make it possible to watch as an extension activity in class. He is a tourism entrepreneur and peace builder. He believes that tourism has the potential of changing people's perspectives as to how they view other cultures.

 **THE DANGER OF A SINGLE STORY**

LESSON OVERVIEW

Aims:
- Watch and understand a talk by author Chimamanda Ngozi Adichie about why it's important to look for varied stories and information about other cultures and people.
- Understand a sequence and a process.
- Identify main events.

TED Talk Summary: In her TED Talk, award-winning novelist Chimamanda Ngozi Adichie shares personal anecdotes about her own life experiences that taught her firsthand how damaging stereotypes can be. She first explains how it wasn't until she started reading books by African writers that she began to finally identify with the stories she wrote as a young child. She next tells us about a boy she knew as a child and her own misinformed beliefs about poverty. She then shares about her move to the U.S. as a university student where she encountered great ignorance about Africans. She then tells how even she needed to relearn this lesson about the dangers of stereotypes once again as an adult in Mexico. Each experience taught her how the images of other cultures and people that we are fed in the media do not tell the whole story. An annotated transcript for the edited TED talk is on pages 86–87 of this Teacher's Guide.

TEACHING NOTES

The paragraph and questions introduce Adichie and her work. The questions encourage students to read this background information and understand more about Adichie, as well as understand more about her concern with stereotypes in literature and the media, which is the topic of her TED Talk. Ask students who have read any of Adichie's books to share about what they read or know about the author. *Extension:* Elicit a discussion about the title of Adiche's talk. What is "a single story" and why is it dangerous?

PART 1

PREVIEWING

Give students a minute to read the paragraph carefully. Have them discuss their ideas in pairs. Play the video to have students check their ideas.

UNDERSTANDING KEY DETAILS

Have students work individually to answer the questions before discussing answers in pairs. *Extension:* Ask partners to talk about the kinds of stories they read and/or wrote as children. Did any of the students have similar experiences to Adichie?

UNDERSTANDING A SEQUENCE OF EVENTS

Have students work alone to complete the activity. Play the video again to have students check their answers. Explain that Adichie is using a series of personal stories from her own history to illustrate how the "single story" can affect people. Ask students to comment on Adichie's personal evolution as a young person. Explain that students will continue to hear about her evolution in Part 2 of the talk. *Extension:* Have students work in pairs to research about an African writer and share what they learned with a small group. Adichie mentions Chinua Achebe and Camara Laye in her talk.

CRITICAL THINKING

Personalizing. Give students a couple of minutes to think about their answers. Encourage them to write notes, perhaps as a concept map, to support their discussion. Then have students work in small groups. Ask them to also talk about how their preference in books and movies has changed over the year. Do they like different things now than when they were younger, or even just a few years ago? Encourage them to think about the connection between their own lives and the stories they read.

PART 2

UNDERSTANDING A PROCESS

Have students look over the chart and questions first before playing the video. Tell them to work individually to answer the questions as they watch. Have them check answers in pairs. Point out that Adichie and Fide are both Nigerian. Elicit a class discussion about stereotypes we have about people in our own countries or cultures and factors that influence that. (religion, race, class, etc.).

IDENTIFYING MAIN IDEAS

A. Give students a few minutes to read the questions and think about and write their answers. Encourage students to write long, thoughtful answers on the lines provided. Point out that Adichie is sharing personal stories to explain her own evolution of thought and experience in regards to both having stereotypes about others and experience others believing stereotypes about her. For question 3, encourage students to think about why Adichie included the story about Mexico in her talk. Students should understand that Adichie is saying that challenging stereotypes is an ongoing and continuous process.

B. Give students time to read the excerpt and think about how to paraphrase what Adichie is saying. Check answers as a class, eliciting reasons that Adichie gives. Ask students to share their opinions about what Adichie says. Do they agree with her? *Extension:* Have students write a personal essay about a time that they stereotyped someone or were stereotyped by someone else.

1. Adichie is a fiction writer from Nigeria. She writes about modern-day African people affected by the legacy of colonialism.; **2.** Her characters are not one-dimensional nor do they play up to stereotypes of Africans. Instead, her characters are interesting, deep, and varied, just as the people of Africa are in reality.; **3.** Answers will vary. Her most recent novel is set in the U.S., not Africa.

PART 1

Previewing

Guesses will vary. Actual answer is: Adichie was mimicking the characters she grew up reading about, which were all Westerners.

Understanding Key Details

1. England and America; **2.** This is what was easily available to her. African books were few and hard to come by.; **3.** She believed that books were about people and places she could not identify with.; **4.** They opened up new worlds for her.

Understanding a Sequence of Events

The following should be in this order: d, e, a, b, c.

Critical Thinking

Personalizing. Answers will vary.

PART 2

Understanding a Process

Preconceived Ideas: the overriding narrative of Fide's family was their poverty

Event that Changed Her Ideas: going to the village, meeting his family, and seeing a basket that his brother had made

New Understanding: more to Fide and his family than the story of poverty

Identifying Main Ideas

A. 1. Her roommate expected someone who could not speak English, who only listened to tribal music, and who could not use a stove.; **2.** Both assumed the other's experiences were limited to poverty; both assumed there was only one dimension to the other.; **3.** When she went to Mexico, she was surprised to encounter Mexicans as people with regular everyday lives. She had heard so many negative things about Mexicans in the U.S. news that she had believed the stereotypes. It wasn't until she visited the country and saw the people there going about their everyday lives that her mind changed.

B. Adichie explains that stereotypes only explain one part of someone's story, and when we believe stereotypes, it emphasizes our differences instead of our similarities as humans.

Critical Thinking

1. Synthesizing. Answers will vary.

2. Relating. Answers will vary.

CRITICAL THINKING

1. Synthesizing. Give students time to think alone before brainstorming in pairs. Note that both Abu Sarah and Adichie fight stereotypes by writing about them. And as TED speakers, they are spreading the message in their speeches, too.

2. Relating. Ask pairs to share with each other a time that they had preconceptions about another person. What happened to make their thinking change?

EXPLORE MORE

Have students also learn more about Adichie's novels. Ask them to choose one and read a short excerpt.

CRITICALLY EVALUATING AN EXAMPLE OF CULTURAL STEREOTYPING

PROJECT OVERVIEW:

Aims:
- Students work in pairs to analyze the portrayal of a fictitious character in relation to culture or country.
- Students describe the character and decide if the portrayal is a stereotype or not.
- Students discuss each other's presentations and share their opinions.

Summary: Students present an analysis of a character from literature, film, or TV. They consider Adichie's concerns about "a single story" as they answer questions together about how the character is represented. They decide whether the portrayal is accurate, a stereotype, or some of both. After each presentation, groups discuss what they learned and share their opinions about the characters.

Materials: computer, Internet access, presentation software or posters and color pens

Language Support: Agreeing or Disagreeing: *I think . . . ; In my opinion, . . . ; I agree because . . . ; I disagree. I think . . .*

TEACHING NOTES

PREPARATION

Ask pairs to brainstorm a list of characters they know from books, movies, or TV that represent a person from a particular culture. Or elicit a class brainstorm and write students' ideas on the board. Encourage pairs to choose characters they are already familiar with. Tell them to use the questions on page 119 to guide their evaluation and analysis. Point out that they should be thinking about Adichie's ideas about "a single story" as they decide together if the character is portrayed fairly or not. Note the "Language Support" phrases above on the board and review them before students begin the activity.

DURING THE PROJECT

Monitor as students prepare their presentations. Remind them that they only have two minutes and so they should think carefully about what information is important to include. Give pairs a few minutes to practice their presentations before dividing the class into groups of three pairs. Make sure each pair in a group is presenting on a different character. While pairs are presenting, remind other group members to listen carefully and take notes.

AFTER THE PROJECT

Tell groups to talk about each of the presentations they saw and to decide what they think about the characters and the analysis. Do they think the pair presented an accurate evaluation? Ask students to share their opinions and discuss where they agree and disagree. ***Extension:*** To encourage further discussion, ask, *How could stereotypes have been avoided in any of these stories?*

EXPLORE MORE

Chevalier wrote the popular novel *The Girl with the Pearl Earring*, which imagines the story behind the famous painting of the same name by Johannes Vermeer. The book was made into a movie in 2003.

PERSONALITY TYPES

UNIT OVERVIEW

Reading: Students read about the author's personal experiences as an introvert and about how society caters to extroverts.

TED Talk: Susan Cain talks about why it's important for society to encourage introverts to be themselves.

Project: Students research and present about the contributions of a famous introvert.

 **PERSONALITY TYPES**

LESSON OVERVIEW

Aims:
- Read and comprehend an essay about how introverted behavior is not always accepted or encouraged in modern society.
- Understand sequence.
- Understand classifications.

Target Vocabulary: colleagues, dominant, emphatically, insights, instill, intuition, longed to be, outgoing, psychologists, solitude

Reading Passage Summary: Students read a personal anecdote about summer camp that explains why the author, a natural introvert, felt that her personality was not accepted easily by others when she was young. She then talks about how she forced herself to be extroverted, even though it was against her natural way of being, until she came to a point in her adult life where she let herself embrace her true personality. In her opinion, society is losing out by trying to make everyone extroverts and by not letting introverts thrive and create in the manner that suits them best.

TEACHING NOTES

THINK AND DISCUSS

The unit explores the idea that society should change its attitude toward introverts. In the last century, society has been built around encouraging extroversion, and author Susan Cain explains in both a personal essay in Lesson A and her TED Talk in Lesson B why society is losing out by not allowing introverts to be themselves. Ask students to look closely at the picture on pages 120–121. Elicit comments about the workplace environment in the picture and students' opinions about the work style that it likely encourages. Ask students to talk about typical workplace environments in their own countries. *Extension:* Note that while an open office like the one pictured does aim to inspire collaboration, at the same time perhaps there are places where people might also be able to get quiet time to work alone. Ask students what they would do in this office if they wanted to work alone.

Think and Discuss

1. Answers will vary. Possibilities include: outgoing, quiet, thoughtful, easygoing, nervous, etc.; **2.** Answers will vary. Open offices like the one pictured usually best suit those who work well in collaborative environments.

Pre-reading

A. 1–3. Answers will vary.

B. Guesses will vary. Her expectation was that there would be a lot of reading and quiet time at camp. In reality, summer camp is often focused on doing various group activities.

Getting the Main Ideas

1. b; **2.** She internalized society's beliefs that extroverts are better.; **3.** Introverts who are forced to operate in a society built for extroverts are not going to be able to produce to their greatest potentials, which in the end negatively affects society.; **4.** She explains that in the quiet moments of alone time is when some people come up with their best ideas. She notes that many of the world's most creative people are also partly introverted.

Understanding Sequence

A. 1. excitement; **2.** confusion; **3.** guilt; **4.** denial

B. The following sentences should be underlined:
excitement: I had this idea that camp was going to be just like this, but better.

confusion: I couldn't figure out for the life of me why we were supposed to be so rowdy, or why we had to spell this word incorrectly.

guilt: I felt kind of guilty about this.

denial: But for years I denied this intuition . . .

Understanding Classifications

A. 1. S; **2.** E; **3.** I; **4.** I

B. 1. solitude/quiet, stimulation/collaboration; **2.** fear social judgment, prefer low-key environments

C. Answers will vary.

Building Vocabulary

A. 1. outgoing; **2.** psychologists; **3.** insight; **4.** solitude

B. 1. d; **2.** f; **3.** e; **4.** a; **5.** c; **6.** b

Getting Meaning from Context

A. 1. mellow; **2.** assertive; **3.** grandiose; **4.** charismatic; **5.** antisocial

B. 1. d; **2.** b; **3.** f; **4.** h; **5.** a; **6.** c; **7.** g; **8.** e

Critical Thinking

1. Inferring. Answers will vary. Cain says that society today believes being extroverted will lead to a more successful life.;
2. Evaluating. Answers will vary.

PRE-READING

A. Give students a minute or so to think about and write their answers before discussing with a partner. Note that the questions aim to have students think about their own levels of introversion by asking them to comment on a group experience. The majority of students may write about positive experiences, since this is the attitude that society encourages toward extroversion and group dynamics. If necessary, have students come back to this activity after they've read the passage to rethink their answers. Did they really have as much fun as they first said they did?

B. Give students a minute to read the first paragraph. Check answers as a class. Explain that the passage is actually a direct excerpt from the first part of Cain's full TED Talk. (In Lesson B, students will view segments from the later part of her talk.) Cain starts with a personal anecdote in order to explain her own natural introversion and how she began to realize that others saw it as unacceptable. The first paragraph shows us that Cain's mistaken image of summer camp was that it would be a place of quiet contemplation with friends nearby, whereas in reality summer camp is centered around group activities and events that encourage extroversion. *Extension:* Have students write a paragraph about what would be an ideal summer camp for them.

DEVELOPING READING SKILLS

GETTING THE MAIN IDEAS

Have students read the entire passage, either silently or while listening to the narrated passage on the audio. Have them work individually to complete the activity before checking answers in pairs. Then have a class discussion to check answers and elicit students' opinions about what Cain says. *Extension:* Tell students to discuss with a partner how they best come up with ideas—by collaborating or by thinking on their own. Ask them to give examples.

UNDERSTANDING SEQUENCE

A. Have students work individually to complete the activity. Tell them to go on to Exercise B without checking answers.

B. Have students work individually to complete Exercise B before checking answers to Exercises A and B in pairs. *Extension:* Ask students to think about an experience when they felt similar emotions. Have them work individually to make a mind map of notes about each feeling and at what point they experienced it. Then have students use their mind maps to tell the story of this experience to a partner.

UNDERSTANDING CLASSIFICATIONS

A. Give students a few minutes to reread the information in the sidebar *Shy or Introverted?* as well as read the description of each person in the activity. Check answers as a class. Elicit any evidence from the sidebar that helped students decide their answers. For example, the sidebar relates shyness to a fear of social judgment. The description of Alex mentions that he worries about what people will think of him, which suggests he is shy rather than introverted.

B. Point out the information for the activity is in the passage sidebar. Have students work individually to complete the activity before checking answers in pairs.

C. Have students discuss in pairs the individuals from Exercise A. Ask students to think about what personality type they are closest to overall, and in what kinds of situations they are shy, introverted, or extroverted. *Extension:* Divide the class into two groups. Have students debate and discuss which they think is a more creative personality type: extrovert or introvert. Tell students to use their own opinions and experiences as well as the information in the passage to support their arguments.

BUILDING VOCABULARY

A. Have students complete Exercise A individually before checking answers as a class. The words *insight* and *outgoing* give a good opportunity to review the meaning of the prefixes *in-* and *out-*. In the word *insight*, the prefix *in-* means within or inner. The noun *insight* means a deep understanding, or inner sight. The prefix *out-* in *outgoing* means to do more than others. To be *outgoing* means to be gregarious, implying that you have more social confidence than most others.

B. Have students complete Exercise B individually before checking answers as a class. If necessary, tell students to find each word in the passage and use context to guess the meaning. *Extension:* Have students write new sentences for each of the vocabulary words in Exercise B.

GETTING MEANING FROM CONTEXT

A. Have students work individually or in pairs to complete Exercises A and B before checking answers as a class.

B. Elicit new example sentences for each word when checking answers as a class. Or have students search for an example sentence with each term online to see the terms in use. *Extension:* Have students write a paragraph about their thoughts on the passage using as many of the terms as possible.

CRITICAL THINKING

1. Inferring. Give students a minute to think about and write their answers in pairs. Then elicit a class discussion to have students share their thoughts. Encourage students to share examples from their home countries.

2. Evaluating. Give students time to think about people they know who support or counter Cain's statement. Have students share their ideas in pairs. Tell them to give examples as they discuss.

EXPLORE MORE

Elicit a discussion about typical TED viewers. For example, it could be argued that since most of the videos are watched online by individuals on their own, it is likely that people who tend to be introverted, who prefer to learn and think alone, are fans of TED.

Lesson 8B THE POWER OF INTROVERTS

LESSON OVERVIEW

Aims:
- Watch and understand a talk about why society needs introverts.
- Understand cause and effect.
- Understand a speaker's message.

TED Talk Summary: In her TED Talk, Susan Cain explains why and how society encourages extroverts instead of introverts. Both schools and offices create environments under the belief system that we're all more productive while in groups and around others. Cain goes back in history to explain how at the turn of the 20th century, the extrovert became the favored personality type when people began living in cities and earning a living by working in business. Her main point is that society is missing out on a lot by not encouraging introverts to be themselves. An annotated transcript for the edited TED Talk is on pages 88–89 of this Teacher's Guide.

TEACHING NOTES

The paragraph introduces the main points of Cain's books, and talks about how popular her talk has been on the TED site. Use these questions to also review what students learned about the power of introverts in Lesson A. For question 2, elicit a class discussion. Ask students to share their ideas about other ways to help introverts succeed. Note that question 3 is an extension of ideas students would have discussed in **Explore More** in Lesson A. *Extension:* Have the class brainstorm some ways that their school or their classroom can be more introvert-friendly.

PART 1

PREVIEWING

Give students a few minutes to work individually to read the paragraph and answer the questions. Play the video before checking answers as a class. For question 1, elicit or explain the figurative language that Cain is using. "Flights of thought" describes letting your mind wander. When it becomes "solo flights," it is thinking and daydreaming piloted only by one person: you. *Extension:* To encourage more discussion, ask students to talk about whether question 2 is true for their home countries as well or not.

UNDERSTANDING KEY DETAILS

Have students work individually to answer the questions. If necessary, play the video again. Cain's point about introverted leaders is that they give their team more freedom to work alone because these leaders understand the benefits of alone time. On the other hand, leaders who are extroverts often try to get too involved in what their teams are doing and control the outcome or even take credit for it. *Extension:* Ask students if they've experienced examples of either of these types of leaders. Have them share their experiences with a partner.

CRITICAL THINKING

Personalizing. Give students a minute to think about their answers before discussing in pairs. Ask students to analyze different offices and school environments that they have experienced, and talk about which ones they enjoyed the most.

PART 2

UNDERSTANDING CAUSE AND EFFECT

Give students time to look over the chart. Play the video. Check answers as a class. Elicit what the cause and effect relationship is in Exercise A. Make sure students understand that Cain talks about how societal changes caused a shift toward favoring extroverts over introverts, and that's why we now have a society that encourages people to be extroverts and discourages introverted behavior.

UNDERSTANDING A SPEAKER'S MESSAGE

Give students two minutes to complete the activity. Note that the statements in the activity are paraphrasing Cain's talk, not verbatim. Have students check answers in pairs. *Extension:* Have students work alone to make a list of both introverted and extroverted activities that they enjoy. Tell them to analyze themselves and determine what percentage of an introvert or extrovert they are.

1. She aimed to show that introverts are important to society.; **2.** She is also giving speeches, such as her TED Talk, about the worth of introverts, and working with a design company to make office furniture for introverted workers.; **3.** Her TED Talk has been viewed over 10 million times, and her book translated into 36 languages.

PART 1

Previewing

1. Answers will vary. Possibilities include: letting your mind wander, spending time alone to think.; **2.** Most classroom situations encourage students to speak up, volunteer, and work well with others. These are all easier for extroverts than introverts.; **3.** Students are forced to interact while they work instead of having quiet time to think and create. The latter is more beneficial for introverted students.

Understanding Key Details

1. Thirty-three to 50 percent of the world population are introverts, according to Cain.; **2.** Schools and offices are both designed to overstimulate people, which is good for extroverts but not introverts.;

3. Introverted leaders tend to try less to control others or become a part of what is happening. Instead, they trust their teams to create and develop ideas.

Critical Thinking

Personalizing. Answers will vary.

PART 2

Understanding Cause and Effect

1. character; **2.** Abraham Lincoln; **3.** big business; **4.** small towns; **5.** big cities; **6.** personality; **7.** salesmen

Understanding a Speaker's Message

1. be themselves, unique solutions; **2.** speaking, attitudes

Critical Thinking

Applying. Answers will vary. Schools and offices could encourage more quiet, reflective time for individuals to work alone. There could also be alternative set ups in offices and classrooms that allow space for solo work as well.

CRITICAL THINKING

Applying. Give students time to think individually before discussing in pairs. Elicit ideas about how the students' school can be changed to be a healthy environment for both introverts and extroverts. Then ask them to comment on the same point for their English classroom. *Extension:* Have pairs draw a design for an introvert-centered office or school environment. Have them present their plans to the class.

EXPLORE MORE

Have students work individually to take the quiz. Then have a class discussion about which questions in the quiz surprised them and why. Ask students to also share if their results surprised them or not and why.

RESEARCHING FOR A PRESENTATION ON CONTRIBUTIONS TO SOCIETY

PROJECT OVERVIEW

Aims:
- Students research and gather information about a famous introvert.
- Students synthesize what they learned in the unit to explain how this person is an introvert, and why it has benefited them and society.
- Students discuss what they learned from each other.

Summary: Students give a brief presentation about a famous introvert who has made a significant contribution to society. Students use what they learned in the unit to support their research and presentation content. The groups discuss each individual presented on and evaluate the presentations.

Materials: access to the Internet, presentation software or poster board and pens

Language Support: Agreeing or Disagreeing: *I think . . . ; I agree because . . . ; I disagree. In my opinion, . . .*

TEACHING NOTES

PREPARATION

Give pairs time to look over the list and choose an individual. Tell them they can also choose another famous introvert that they know about who is not on the list. Monitor students' choices to make sure that a variety of individuals are represented overall. Explain that students should use the questions on page 135 to guide their research. Ask them to especially think about whether the individual's introversion has helped or hindered their success, and how. Note the "Language Support" phrases above on the board and review them before students begin the activity.

DURING THE PROJECT

Monitor as students prepare their presentations. Remind them that they only have two minutes, and so they should think carefully about what information is important to include. Encourage students to use images or video to support their presentations. Give pairs a few minutes to practice their presentations before dividing the class into groups of three pairs. While pairs are presenting, remind other group members to listen carefully and take notes.

AFTER THE PROJECT

After each pair has presented, tell groups to use their notes to discuss each famous introvert further. Tell group members to explain what they learned from each other and share what they want to know more about. Give students time to tell even more about their individuals if there was content they weren't able to include in the two minutes of the presentation.
Extension: Elicit a class discussion by asking students to talk about how their views about introverts have changed during the unit.

EXPLORE MORE

Encourage students to learn from each other about introversion and extroversion in different cultures. Or have students go online to learn about it and report back to the class or their groups.

SMART THINKING

UNIT OVERVIEW

Reading: Students are introduced to new ways in which researchers are learning to communicate with animals.

TED Talk: Primatologist Susan Savage-Rumbaugh talks about her work building an intelligent community of humans and bonobos.

Project: Students present a proposal to get research funding to study more about animal intelligence.

 **THE NATURE OF INTELLIGENCE**

LESSON OVERVIEW

Aims:
- Read and comprehend an article about what the latest research in animal intelligence is teaching us about the capabilities of other species.
- Infer conclusions.
- Understand references.

Target Vocabulary: abstract, adept at, capable, contrary, correspond to, integrate, intrigued by, remarkable, resonated, superior

Reading Passage Summary: Students read about new insights into animal intelligence coming from various interesting research projects. In some cases, we are finding that animals are actually quicker to pick up our ways of communication than we are to pick up theirs, which challenges preconceptions about human superiority. With the help of music and computers, scientists and researchers are seeing that animals not only mimic, but respond with their own unique thoughts and communications.

TEACHING NOTES

THINK AND DISCUSS

This unit takes a closer look at animal intelligence, introducing current research that challenges preconceptions about the limitation of what animals can do cognitively. Have students work in pairs to discuss the questions, or elicit a class discussion. Ask students to give examples to support their ideas. For question 1, elicit any stories that students have of witnessing or experiencing animal communication. Encourage students to explore their own preconceptions about animal versus human intelligence in question 2. After they've completed the entire unit, come back to the second part of question 2 to ask if students' opinions have changed.

PRE-READING

A. Have students answer questions individually before discussing answers in pairs. Note that question 1 only refers to the pictures of the dolphins and the elephant. Extend the question to include the chimpanzee on

Think and Discuss

1. Answers will vary. Possibilities include: making sounds, eye contact, touching, physical play, etc.; **2.** Answers will vary.

Pre-reading

A. 1. Answers will vary.; **2.** Answer will vary. Possibilities include: octopus, squid, whales, pigs, parrots, horses, etc.

B. Answers will vary. Studying animal intelligence gives us insight into the animal brain, as well as teaches us about human intelligence.

C. Answers will vary. Music and the Internet both offer exciting, alternate ways of establishing communication with animals.

Getting the Main Ideas

1. d; **2.** e; **3.** a; **4.** c; **5.** b

Understanding Key Details

A. a. Paragraph 8; **b.** Paragraph 7; **c.** Paragraph 6; **d.** Paragraphs 1–2; **e.** Paragraphs 3–4

B. Groups of humpback whales sing similar songs, and songs vary between groups and by region, just as human language does. Yet each whale's song is slightly individualized and original, as is human communication. However, unlike human communication, whales sing the same song repeatedly.

C. 1. a, c, d; **2.** a, d

Inferring Conclusions

1. b; **2.** a; **3.** c

Building Vocabulary

A. 1. a; **2.** a; **3.** c; **4.** c; **5.** d

B. 1. capable; **2.** contrary; **3.** abstract; **4.** remarkable; **5.** integrate

C. 1. Answers will vary.; **2.** Answers will vary.

Getting Meaning from Context

1. b; **2.** Interfaces can provide ways to understand how the animal mind functions by giving us opportunities to interact with them more.; **3.** Answers will vary. Possibilities include: computers connected to the Internet, telephones and cell phones, forums online for chatting, social media sites, a break room or social room at work or school, etc.

Understanding Reference

1. a; **2.** a; **3.** b

Critical Thinking

Applying. Answers will vary. The passage implies that when we find more effective ways to communicate with animals, we will better understand their true intelligence and not be so quick to consider ours to be superior. Once we are able to understand animals better, we will also start learning from them, and our attitudes about them may change considerably.

---

page 137 and the whales on page 141 if you want students to have more options to discuss. For question 2, have the class brainstorm a list of species that are considered highly intelligent. *Extension:* Have students work in pairs to search online to find out more about one species of intelligent animals. Ask them to present what they learned to the class. Note that students can use this as background information later during the **Project**.

B. Give students time to think about their ideas and write them down before discussing in pairs. Encourage students to think about what humans can learn from animals.

C. Encourage students to work individually or in pairs to make a concept map or Venn diagram to brainstorm ideas and connections between animals, music, and

the Internet. *Extension:* Ask students to share with the class or a partner any interesting or unusual experiences they've had communicating with animals.

DEVELOPING READING SKILLS

GETTING THE MAIN IDEAS

Have students read the entire passage, either silently or while listening to the narrated passage on the audio. Have them work individually to answer the questions for Exercise A before checking answers in pairs. *Extension:* Have students choose one of the experts mentioned in the passage and find out more online about that individual's work with animals or theories about animal intelligence.

UNDERSTANDING KEY DETAILS

A. Give students one to two minutes to go back to the passage and find the information. Have them work individually to complete Exercise A before checking answers as a class. Then elicit the answers for each of the questions. *Extension:* Assign pairs one of the questions to answer in their own words without looking back at the passage again. Have them tell the class. Ask the class to then check their classmates' answers.

B. Give students time to reread the sidebar, if necessary, and think about their answers. Have them work individually to answer the question. Elicit a class discussion to check answers. When discussing the whales, encourage students to think about how their native languages vary in their own countries in areas such as dialect and region.

C. Have students work individually to complete the activity before checking answers as a class. Ask students to share their thoughts about what Reiss and Gabriel learned while interacting with animals. *Extension:* Ask students to comment on the form of animal communication that they read about in the passage that surprised them most, and why.

INFERRING CONCLUSIONS

Explain that each of the quotations in the activity implies a conclusion that supports one of the author's main ideas. Point out that writers often use expert quotations to indirectly communicate their thesis to readers. Ask students to comment on why this is a useful strategy. Make sure they understand that expert quotations help add believability to what a writer is saying. Have students work individually to complete the activity before checking answers in pairs. *Extension:* Have pairs choose one conclusion from the activity and discuss it in more detail. Do they agree with it?

BUILDING VOCABULARY

A. Have students complete Exercise A individually before checking answers as a class. If students need further support, tell them to substitute the answer choices for the word in the sentence to check which definition sounds most logical. Note that while *correspond to* can also mean *match,* students should recognize from context that the symbols on the keyboard are activating various interactions for the dolphins, which is why they are motivated to engage with the keyboard. When something *resonates with* something else, it agrees with it. Reiss's findings were similar to others' also working with animals.

B. Have students complete Exercise B individually before checking answers in pairs. Ask students to explain in their own words the meaning of *self-aware* and *abstract thought*. *Extension:* Elicit ideas about what an interspecies Internet might be like.

C. Give students a minute to think about their answers individually before discussing in pairs. Then elicit a class discussion, asking pairs to share one or two points that they talked about. *Extension:* Have students work individually to write answers to one of the questions in the activity, using as many vocabulary words as they can.

GETTING MEANING FROM CONTEXT

Have students work individually to complete the activity before checking answers as a class. Note that creating *interfaces* is the main idea behind the research being talked about in the passage. Make sure students understand that an interface is a platform for interaction or communication. Students might be familiar with the term as used to describe apps or programs that allow us to use computers and interact online. For question 3, have pairs share some ideas with the class. *Extension:* Ask students to think about how some of these everyday interfaces could be used to connect with animals. Have them discuss in pairs.

UNDERSTANDING REFERENCE

Explain that one reason writers use pronouns is to add variety to their sentences, so they are not writing the same nouns over and over again. Point out that in content like the reading passage, where both experts and animals are constantly talked about, it is important for the context to make it clear which one the pronoun is referring to. Have students work individually to complete the activity before checking answers in pairs. *Extension:* Have students work in pairs to find sentences with pronouns in reading passages in past units. Ask them to pick up sentences and have their partners identify the reference.

CRITICAL THINKING

Applying. Give students a minute to think about their answers before discussing in pairs or small groups. Tell students to give examples and reasons to support their ideas and explain their experiences. Ask students who have pets to talk about how their interactions and relationship with the animal might or might not change if they could understand each other better. *Extension:* Have students work in small groups to design a new interface for communicating with dolphins, bonobos, elephants, or whales. Have them present their interfaces to the class or another group.

Note that the details in the passage students read in Lesson A come mostly from the TED Talk "The interspecies Internet." Students will be familiar with some of the content when they watch it and get the chance to learn more details about each expert's research and ideas.

Lesson 9B THE GENTLE GENIUS OF BONOBOS

LESSON OVERVIEW

Aims:

- Watch and understand a talk about how a research team is interacting with, teaching, and learning from a community of bonobos.
- Understand a speaker's message.
- Understand sequence.

TED Talk Summary: In her TED Talk, primatologist Susan Savage-Rumbaugh explains and shares video of the research she is doing with a community of scientists and bonobos. She shows what humanlike things bonobos have learned to do, ranging from communicating with symbols to driving a golf cart. As she shows us these images, she challenges our thinking about human superiority and inferior animal intelligence. After her years of work with bonobos, Savage-Rumbaugh believes that social environment and culture affect evolution more than biology. An annotated transcript for the edited TED Talk is on pages 90–92 of this Teacher's Guide.

TEACHING NOTES

The paragraph and questions provide background information on the TED speaker and her work. Have students work individually to complete the activity. Check answers as a class, using question 3 to encourage a discussion about preconceptions that humans have about animal intelligence. Encourage students to use their background knowledge from Lesson A to help them predict the answers to the questions. Point out that Savage-Rumbaugh is both a primatologist and psychologist. Ask students to comment on how these two professions might help her in her research. **Extension:** Have students work in pairs to search online to learn more about the bonobos species before watching the TED Talk.

PART 1

PREVIEWING

Give students two minutes to work individually to write their lists before comparing ideas with a partner. Tell students to think of things they can do that they don't think animals can. Elicit a class discussion to hear students' ideas. **Extension:** Have students write a short essay about how their preconceptions about animal intelligence have changed so far in the unit. Then have them revisit the essay when they have completed the unit to see if their ideas have changed any more.

UNDERSTANDING MAIN IDEAS

Have students read the questions. Play the video. Check answers as a class. For question 1, elicit an explanation of each of the aspects of intelligence, and why we usually consider it to be special to humans. *Causal thought* refers to recognizing cause-and-effect relationships between events and using this to problem-solve and understand what is happening around you. Ask students to comment on why Savage-Rumbaugh specifies: "None of the things you will see in this particular video are trained." **Extension:** Have students share in pairs which action by a bonobo in the video surprised them the most, and why.

UNDERSTANDING A SPEAKER'S MESSAGE

A. Have students work individually to complete the activity. Play the video again for students to check answers. As they watch, tell them to also think about their answers to Exercise B.

B. Give students a minute to work individually to write their answers before checking answers as a class. Make sure students understand that each phrase aims to attribute what we otherwise consider human characteristics to the behavior of the bonobos in the video.

1. She studied bonobos and chimpanzees. Her goal is to find out more about their cognitive and linguistic abilities.; **2.** Answers may vary. It is likely that the behaviors demonstrate causal thought or the ability to make tools.; **3.** If animals can learn to demonstrate skills that we consider uniquely human, it may mean that human development has been shaped more by social environment than biology and that humans are not so superior after all.

PART 1

Previewing

Answers will vary. Possibilities include: abstract thought, humor, walking upright on two legs, using an opposable thumb, etc.

Understanding Main Ideas

1. causal thought, language, (the ability to) make tools, mathematics
2. **a.** lighter, fire; **b.** drive (a golf cart); **c.** herself in a mirror; **d.** scissors, hair; **e.** tools, rocks

Understanding a Speaker's Message

A. 1. b; **2.** d; **3.** c; **4.** a

B. Savage-Rumbaugh is pointing out similarities in the behaviors of humans and bonobos.

PART 2

Previewing

A. The purpose of the research is to see how bonobos and humans influence each other. It is aiming to prove that culture and social surroundings are what help us evolve, not biology.

Understanding Sequence

1. communicate; **2.** symbols; **3.** draw; **4.** shape; **5.** represents; **6.** writing

Understanding Key Details

A. The following should be checked: use language around them, create a relaxed and fun environment, interact with people who are important to them.

B. When a language is acquired, it is learned organically as part of being surrounded by it. When a language is taught, it is learned by studying it.

Critical Thinking

Reflecting. Answers will vary.

PART 2

PREVIEWING

A. Give students a minute to read the paragraph and write the purpose of Savage-Rumbaugh's research. Tell them to paraphrase what the paragraph says in their own words.

B. Play the video for students to check their answers. Elicit the meaning of *bi-species environment*.
Extension: Ask students to discuss or write about how the researchers are becoming like the bonobos, according to Savage-Rumbaugh.

UNDERSTANDING SEQUENCE

Have students work individually to complete the activity before checking answers in pairs. Elicit students' impressions of what they saw Panbanisha do to express herself. *Extension:* Have students work in small groups to retell what they saw Panbanisha do in the video. Explain that each group member will explain one part of the sequence in their own words. Then the next group member will explain the next part, and so on.

UNDERSTANDING KEY DETAILS

A. Give students a few minutes to work individually to read the paragraph and complete the activity before checking answers as a class. Elicit a class discussion about the three situations that have helped the bonobos acquire language. Do students think that these points also apply to their own language learning?

B. Have students discuss their answers in pairs. Then elicit their ideas, asking for reasons and examples.

CRITICAL THINKING

Reflecting. Give students time to think about their answer to the question. Point out that the question asks about first language, which is most likely also their native language. Students should understand that they should reflect on how they learned language organically as a baby. Have students discuss in pairs, giving examples of personal experiences. *Extension:* Have students write an opinion essay about whether or not they agree with Savage-Rumbaugh's ideas about language acquisition.

PROPOSING AND JUSTIFYING A WILDLIFE RESEARCH PROJECT

PROJECT OVERVIEW:

Aims:
- Students work in groups to watch a TED Talk and write a proposal for research funding.
- Students outline their research plan and create a presentation about it with a graphic organizer.
- Students decide which proposal has the most benefits.

Summary: Students create a research project on animal intelligence for which they need to find funding. Groups present their research projects to others to ask for funding. The class decides which projects they want to support.

Materials: computer and printer, poster board and pens, or presentation software

Language Support: Using persuasive language: *Some of the benefits include . . . ; The reason this is important is . . . ; We strongly believe that . . .*

TEACHING NOTES

PREPARATION

Have students work in groups of three. Give them time to search online briefly at TED.com to read the summary of each talk. Then ask them to choose one to watch. As students watch, tell them to take notes on the animals and the research being done. Note that students can also find their own species by doing online research. Tell students to think like grant writers as they research, and find the key points that will be easy to explain to others when asking for financial support.

Encourage them to use the points in question 2 when creating content for their presentation. Note the "Language Support" phrases on the board and review them before students begin the activity.

DURING THE PROJECT

Have groups work together to create their proposals. Remind them that their goal is to justify their projects and convince others to support it. Point out that they should try to use persuasive language to win the votes of their audience. If students make posters, give them time to draw pictures and add information about the research and its purpose. Monitor as students work together to create their proposals. Give assistance or feedback when necessary. Let groups practice once before presenting to the class. As students present, remind those who are listening to take notes and think about which project they think is most worthy of support.

AFTER THE PROJECT

Elicit a class discussion about the presentations. Give students time to have a question-and-answer session about the presentations if necessary. Then take a class vote to decide which of the projects students want to support. Ask students to comment on why they chose that project to support.

EXPLORE MORE

If time permits, have students read the article before their presentations to help make their proposals stronger.

Unit 10

FACING FEAR

UNIT OVERVIEW

Reading: Students read about how astronauts train for life-threatening situations.

TED Talk: Astronaut Chris Hadfield shares what he's learned about overcoming fear while in space.

Project: Students create a training course to help people overcome specific phobias.

 **KEEP CALM!**

LESSON OVERVIEW

Aims:
- Read and comprehend an article about how astronauts are trained to deal with emergencies in space and the fear that comes with them.
- Link ideas and examples.
- Create a map of the text.
- Understand a process.

Target Vocabulary: conduct, countless, detaching, emergencies, exposure, irrational, malfunction, overcoming, stranded, unpredictable

Reading Passage Summary: Students read about the dangers that astronauts may face in space and how they are trained to deal with both the physical and mental aspects of this. Overcoming fear is especially important, as it keeps the astronauts calm and able to deal with the crisis at hand. The way in which astronauts train to deal with the feeling of fear can also be useful in everyday life to people with phobias. It is believed that a slow progression of repeated practice and repeated exposure to a phobia shifts the behavior, and therefore the fear, in relation to it.

TEACHING NOTES

THINK AND DISCUSS

This unit talks about how fear affects us and what can be done to overcome the feeling. Have students discuss question 1 in pairs. Encourage them to think about everyday fears they face as well as talk about any phobias, or extreme fears, that they have. For question 2, elicit a class discussion to brainstorm a list of dangerous jobs. Ask students to comment on which jobs they might want to try and why.

PRE-READING

A. Make sure students understand that *phobia* means an extreme fear. Have students work in pairs to brainstorm a list of common phobias. Elicit ideas to check answers as a class. Ask students to share if they have any phobias.

B. Give students a minute to look over the list and think about anyone they know with phobias. Have them work individually to write their answers before sharing with a partner. Encourage students to use

Think and Discuss

1. Answers will vary.; **2.** Answers will vary. Possibilities include: astronauts, police, firefighters, coal miners, sailors, construction workers, sewage cleaners, people who work with explosives, etc. Dangerous jobs are often high-paying, which may attract some people. Other people enjoy the adrenaline rush or excitement experienced during frightening situations.

Pre-reading

A. Answers will vary. See list on page 156.

B. Answers will vary.

C. Answers will vary. Possibilities include: the launch and trip into space, living without gravity, facing dangers on spacewalks (such as having a problem with a spacesuit or getting detached from the space station).

D. b

Getting the Main Ideas

A. b, c

B. The following should be checked: a, c, g.

Linking Ideas and Examples

A. 1. b; **2.** c; **3.** e

Creating a Map of the Text

1. spacesuit; **2.** water (in helmet); **3.** spaceship;
4. spacewalks; **5.** space station; **6.** mini-jetpacks;
7. questions; **8.** feared situation; **9.** easy situations;
10. challenging ones

Getting Meaning from Context

1–3. Answers may vary slightly. Possibilities include:
1. hole / deep cut; **2.** water out / out water; **3.** scary / dangerous / worrisome / important

Building Vocabulary

A. 1. a; **2.** d; **3.** a; **4.** c; **5.** d

B. 1. emergency; **2.** malfunction; **3.** detach;
4. overcome; **5.** exposure

Understanding a Process

1. b; **2.** increases the level of anxiety, gradually adapt to more stressful situations

Critical Thinking

1. Questioning. Parmitano is saying that the primary goal of astronauts is to visit and learn about space, not to adapt to living there. He is pointing out that space is an environment not suited to humans, and there are many unknowns and dangers that astronauts experience and encounter while out in this very far away and very foreign place.

2. Applying. Answers will vary.

examples and stories. Point out that students can also talk about themselves.

C. Have students work individually to answer the question before checking answers as a class. Make a mind map on the board of students' answers.
Extension: Ask students to comment on whether they think they could be an astronaut or not, and why.

D. Give students 30 seconds to quickly skim the passage and complete the activity. Check answers as a class. Elicit any clues students picked up while skimming to help them answer the question.

DEVELOPING READING SKILLS

GETTING THE MAIN IDEAS

A. Have students work individually to complete the activity before checking answers as a class. Point out that while the fear ladder is discussed in the article and introduced in the infographic, the author does not directly state that astronauts use it to overcome fears.

B. Have students work individually to complete the activity before checking answers in pairs. Ask students to identify what purpose the statements that are not main ideas serve. They are examples that support the main ideas in the passage. Students will look at these more closely in the next activity.

LINKING IDEAS AND EXAMPLES

Give students a minute to read each example and find the key idea it illustrates. Have students check answers in pairs. *Extension:* Have partners find one or two more examples from the passage and ask each other to identify the main idea with which it links.

CREATING A MAP OF THE TEXT

Explain that creating a map of the information in a passage can be a helpful way to summarize, a skill that is both useful and necessary in researching and reviewing texts. Point out that the diagram contains key points from the reading. Have students work individually or in pairs to complete the details. *Extension:* Make completing the map a race between partners or pairs.

GETTING MEANING FROM CONTEXT

Tell students to use only the quotes on the page to guess the meaning of the words. Have them work individually before checking their answers in pairs. Then elicit clues that helped students find the correct definition. Note that the word *puncture* is commonly used to talk about a hole in a bicycle or car tire that lets out the air. Something can *leak* air, water, gas, or any other substance contained in it. The use of the word in the passage refers to an accidental leak. The colloquialism "It's not a big deal" is often used to tell someone to calm down or encourage them to think more rationally about a situation.

BUILDING VOCABULARY

A. Have students complete Exercise A individually before checking answers in pairs. Explain that the prefix *ir-* in *irrational* is a variant of the prefix *in-*, which students are likely familiar with. Both prefixes mean "not." Other variants include *il-* and *im-*. Examples include: *irrelevant, invalid, illegal, impossible.* Something that is described as *countless* is too big to count. The suffix *-less* means "without." Examples include: *nameless, formless, thoughtless,* etc.

B. Have students complete Exercise B individually before checking answers in pairs. When you *overcome* something, you successfully deal with it or get over an obstacle. However, another meaning of the verb, often seen as *be overcome,* is to be overpowered or feel overwhelmed. *Extension:* Have students work alone to write a story about overcoming fear. Tell them to use as many vocabulary words as possible.

UNDERSTANDING A PROCESS

Give students a few minutes to closely read the infographic on page 157. Have them work individually to answer the questions before checking answers in pairs. Elicit a summary of how the ladder works. *Extension:* Have students work as a class or in pairs to outline the steps in the fear ladder. Make sure not to use any of the phobias listed on page 157 for the **Project.** Alternately, have students do the activity in groups with the topics for the **Project** and use it as background for the poster they will make.

CRITICAL THINKING

1. **Questioning.** Give students a minute to think about their answers before discussing in pairs. Tell students to think and discuss about the differences between explorers and colonizers, especially in regards to mindset, preparation, and information. Ask students to talk about whether they think humans today could be successful colonizers in space. Why or why not?

2. **Applying.** Give students a minute to look back at their answers to the **Pre-reading** and to think about that person in regards to the fear ladder. Then ask them to explain to their partner the steps that the person should take to overcome the fear. *Extension:* Ask students to analyze and offer their opinions about the fear ladder approach. Do they think it works in all cases? What are some phobias that the fear ladder might not work for?

EXPLORE MORE

Ask students to brainstorm ways in which regular people might quickly train to go into space if one day commercial flights are made available.

WHAT I LEARNED FROM GOING BLIND IN SPACE

LESSON OVERVIEW

Aims:
- Watch and understand a talk about how overcoming an emergency in space gave an astronaut a new perspective on fear.
- Interpret descriptions.
- Understand a sequence of events.

TED Talk Summary: In his TED Talk, astronaut Chris Hadfield talks about the risky and dangerous situations that astronauts must be able to get through during their space missions, from taking off in a rocket at high speeds, to accelerating through space, to living on a station orbiting the Earth, to going on spacewalks. In every situation, an astronaut is one misstep away from a fatality, which is why they train so vigorously. Hadfield tells a story of going temporarily blind on a spacewalk, and what it taught him about perceived danger versus real danger. An annotated transcript for the edited TED Talk is on pages 93–95 of this Teacher's Guide.

TEACHING NOTES

The paragraphs tell us more about Hadfield's career as an astronaut and how he tries to share with the public about his experiences and what those experiences have taught him. The information will build on what students learned about Hadfield's ideas in Lesson A. Have students read the paragraphs individually before writing their answers. Tell them to use what they learned in Lesson A in their answers. Check answers as a class. *Extension:* Have students work in pairs or small groups to go online and find Hadfield's social media account or Twitter page to read some of his past posts, as well as comments from his audience. What are some topics he talks about?

PART 1

PREVIEWING

Have students work individually to read the paragraph and answer the questions before checking answers in pairs. If necessary, elicit or explain the meaning of *shuttle launch* and *catastrophic*. *Extension:* Point out that Hadfield is saying that a dangerous situation is a scary one. Ask students if they can think of any exceptions.

UNDERSTANDING MAIN IDEAS

Have students read the questions. Then play the video. Have students check answers in pairs. For question 3, elicit a class discussion about what Hadfield says. Note that students' answers may vary depending how they interpret the word *perspective*. Hadfield says that being in space gives him a literal new perspective on the planet because he can look down on it and see how beautiful it is, but he also talks about a bigger shift in his thinking in understanding more deeply his connection to the world, its people, and our place in the vast universe.

INTERPRETING DESCRIPTIONS

A. Give students a few minutes to carefully read the excerpts and complete the activity. Have them check answers in pairs. Elicit the meanings of the figurative language that Hadfield uses in the excerpts: "in the jaws of some enormous dog," "like someone's pouring cement on you," "a self-propelled art gallery," "with a texture you feel like you could stick your hand into."

B. Give students time to work individually to look over the feelings listed and go back to the excerpts in Exercise A. Tell them to think about how to support their answers with examples or explanations. Have students discuss their answers in pairs. Encourage them to add other feelings to the list. *Extension:* Elicit any additional feelings that pairs come up with. Ask for the terms only. Then have the other students in the class decide which excerpt this word is relevant for, and why.

CRITICAL THINKING

Interpreting. Give students a few minutes to think and write their ideas individually first. Students should recognize that there is some humor involved in this statement. If necessary, explain the colloquial meaning of *jaw-dropping*. See **Answer Key**.

PART 2

RECOGNIZING MAIN IDEAS

Have students read the questions and answer choices. Then play the video. Check answers as a class. Hadfield talks about having practiced a variety of specific situations, so students should be able to infer that losing his vision was one of them.

1. A person with a sense of tenacity and purpose, not someone who is wishy-washy. Someone who handles fear well.; **2.** by practicing repeatedly and exposing himself to various worst-case scenarios

PART 1

Previewing

The following should be checked: b, f.

Understanding Main Ideas

1. when as a boy he watched the first astronauts walk on the moon; **2.** to go outside on a spacewalk; **3.** He says that seeing the world from space literally changed the way he understood its beauty. He also talks about being outside on a spacewalk and recognizing how he is a part of the universe, just as Earth is, and feeling how delicate and real his physical connection is to Earth and other humans.

Interpreting Descriptions

A. the view of Earth from space: d; the experience of taking a spacewalk: e; the International Space Station: c; being inside a rocket as it starts to lift off: a; the view of deep space from outside the spacecraft: f; feeling a rocket's acceleration: b

B. Answers may vary. Possibilities include: a sense of awe, astonishment, fascination, powerlessness, joy.

Critical Thinking

Interpreting. Hadfield is referring to being in a place with zero gravity—your jaw physically cannot drop. The expression *jaw-dropping* is used to describe a feeling of great surprise and sometimes awe or wonder, which is what he felt when he saw Earth from above.

PART 2

Recognizing Main Ideas

1. a; **2.** b

Understanding a Sequence of Events

A. from top to bottom: 4, 3, 6, 1, 7, 8, 2, 9, 5 **or** 6, 3, 5, 1, 7, 8, 2, 9, 4

B. The following should be checked: b, d, e, g, h.

Explore More

Hadfield realized that fear becomes less of an obstacle in life when it's dealt with rationally through recognizing the difference between real and perceived danger.

UNDERSTANDING A SEQUENCE OF EVENTS

A. Give students a few minutes to put the events in the correct sequence before checking answers in pairs. Note that there are two possible sequences: Hadfield mentions twice that he continues working (item a), first after he didn't know what to do, then after he goes completely blind. Elicit answers, writing a timeline on the board of the events Hadfield describes. *Extension:* Ask students to talk about at what point in the timeline of events they think they would have panicked.

B. Have students work in pairs to complete the activity before checking answers as a class. Elicit students' thoughts about what Hadfield experienced and how he kept himself calm. *Extension:* Ask students to share with a partner which thought that went through Hadfield's head would have calmed them the most, and why.

EXPLORE MORE

Encourage students to also find excerpts online from Hadfield's book, *An Astronaut's Guide to Life on Earth.*

DESIGNING A 3-DAY COURSE FOR TACKLING PHOBIAS

PROJECT OVERVIEW

Aims:
- Students work in small groups to design a training course for overcoming fears.
- Students synthesize what they learned in the unit to create a useful course.
- Teams present their training courses to the class.

Summary: Students design a three-day training program for people overcoming a specific phobia. Groups work together to decide what activities participants will do and how they will gradually climb the fear ladder over the three days. Groups present their training courses to the class, explaining in detail how participants will meet with success after three days.

Materials: computer, presentation software, poster board and colored pens

Language Support: Presentation language: *Today I am going to introduce . . . ; Let me first explain . . . ; Let's next talk about . . .*

TEACHING NOTES

PREPARATION

Have students work in groups of three. Ask them to look over the list of fears and choose one for their course. Encourage them to quickly discuss some possible ideas, and to think about which course they'd most enjoy designing. Monitor choices to make sure that a variety of fears are represented in the presentations. Tell students to use the points on page 167 to help them plan their courses. Tell group members to each contribute their opinions and ideas. Note the "Language Support" phrases above on the board and review them before students begin the activity.

DURING THE PROJECT

Give students enough time to make the posters for their presentations. Explain that they should create a detailed fear ladder that explains how participants in their course will overcome their fears. Tell groups to make sure that each member has an equal role in the presentation. Encourage members to speak for two minutes each, for a total of six minutes per group, if time permits. Monitor as groups work on their presentations. Give assistance or feedback when necessary. Give groups time for members to practice their parts for each other and get feedback before presenting to the class.

AFTER THE PROJECT

When groups present, remind the students listening to be respectful and to be active listeners who take notes and think of questions during the presentations. After all groups have presented, ask the class to discuss the different courses presented. Encourage students to offer feedback to each other with ideas on how to make their courses better. Encourage them to give reasons and examples for their opinions about the courses. **Extension:** Have students vote on which program they think is most likely to help someone overcome the intended fear in three days.

EXPLORE MORE

Make sure students who choose fear of flying for their presentation topic do not check this website ahead of time. Encourage groups to use only their original ideas, supported by the background information they learned in the unit, when designing their courses.

TEDTALK ANNOTATED VIDEO TRANSCRIPTS

Unit 1 **LOUIE SCHWARTZBERG**

Hidden Miracles of the Natural World

Part 1

What is the intersection between technology, art, and science? Curiosity and wonder, because it **drives us**[1] to explore, because we're surrounded by things we can't see. And I love to use film to take us on a journey through portals of time and space, to make the invisible visible, because what that does, it **expands our horizons**,[2] it transforms our perception, it opens our minds and it touches our heart. So here are some scenes from my 3-D **IMAX**[3] film, *Mysteries of the Unseen World*.[4]

There is movement which is too slow for our eyes to detect, and time-lapse makes us discover and broaden our perspective of life. We can see how organisms emerge and grow, how a vine survives by creeping from the forest floor to look at the sunlight. And at the **grand scale**,[5] time-lapse allows us to see our planet in motion. We can view not only the vast sweep of nature, but the restless movement of humanity. Each streaking dot represents a **passenger plane**,[6] and by turning air traffic data into time-lapse imagery, we can see something that's above us constantly but invisible: the vast network of air travel over the United States. We can do the same thing with ships at sea. We can turn data into a time-lapse view of a global economy in motion. And decades of data give us the view of our entire planet as a single organism sustained by currents circulating throughout the oceans and by clouds swirling through the atmosphere, pulsing with lightning, crowned by the aurora borealis. It may be the ultimate time-lapse image: the anatomy of Earth **brought to life**.[7]

At the other extreme,[8] there are things that move too fast for our eyes, but we have technology that can look into that world as well. With high-speed cameras, we can do the opposite of time-lapse. We can shoot images that are thousands of times faster than our vision. And we can see how nature's ingenious devices work, and perhaps we can even imitate them. When a dragonfly flutters by, you may not realize, but it's the greatest flyer in nature. It can hover, fly backwards, even upside down. And by tracking markers on an insect's wings, we can visualize the air flow that they produce. Nobody knew the secret, but high-speed shows that a dragonfly can move all four wings in different directions at the same time. And what we learn can lead us to new kinds of **robotic flyers**[9] that can expand our vision of important and remote places.

Part 2

We're **giants**,[10] and we're unaware of things that are too small for us to see. The **electron microscope**[11] fires electrons which creates images which can magnify things by

---

[1] Something that "drives you," motivates and compels you to take a specific action.

[2] The term "expand [someone's] horizons" refers to introducing new ideas that open a person's mind.

[3] The IMAX film format lets large-size movies be made with images of a higher resolution than what is typical.

[4] *Mysteries of the Unseen World* came out in 2013. It was a 3-D IMAX film.

[5] The "grand scale" refers to the bigger perspective or purpose.

[6] A "passenger plane" is any plane that carries people instead of things.

[7] The phrase "brought to life" means to animate something or create relevance for it with others.

[8] Something that is "on the other extreme" is on the other side of a spectrum based on a topic previously spoken about. The phrase is a way to introduce an opposing subject, but one that is connected to the original topic.

[9] The "robotic flyers" that Schwartzberg is referring to are likely drones used for research.

[10] Humans are called "giants" to show how small many other living organisms actually are.

[11] An "electron microscope" uses electron beams and high magnification, allowing it to see very tiny things in greater detail.

as much as a million times. This is the egg of a butterfly. And there are unseen creatures living all over your body, including mites that spend their entire lives dwelling on your eyelashes, crawling over your skin at night. Can you guess what this is? Shark skin. A caterpillar's mouth. The eye of a fruit fly. An eggshell. A flea. A snail's tongue. We think we know most of the animal kingdom, but there may be millions of tiny species waiting to be discovered.

A spider also has great secrets, because spider's silk thread is **pound for pound**[12] stronger than steel but completely elastic. This journey will take us all the way down to the nano world. The silk is 100 times thinner than human hair. On there is bacteria, and near that bacteria, 10 times smaller, a virus. Inside of that, 10 times smaller, three strands of DNA, and **nearing the limit**[13] of our most powerful microscopes, single carbon atoms.

With the tip of a powerful microscope, we can actually move atoms and begin to create amazing nano devices. Some could **one day**[14] patrol our body for all kinds of diseases and clean out clogged arteries along the way. Tiny chemical machines of the future can one day, perhaps, repair DNA. We are **on the threshold**[15] of extraordinary advances, born of our drive to unveil the mysteries of life.

So under an endless rain of cosmic dust, the air is full of pollen, micro-diamonds, and jewels from other planets, and supernova explosions. People **go about their lives**[16] surrounded by the unseeable. Knowing that there's so much around us we can see forever changes our understanding of the world, and by looking at unseen worlds, we recognize that we exist in the living universe, and this new perspective creates wonder and inspires us to become explorers in our own backyards.

Who knows what awaits to be seen and what new wonders will transform our lives? We'll just have to see.

Thank you.

---

[12] The phrase "pound for pound" is used to show the value of someone or something in relation to size. It is commonly used to talk about sport fighters, such as boxers.

[13] When something "nears the limit," it is almost at the end of what it's capable of doing.

[14] The term "one day" is commonly used to talk about an unspecified time in the future.

[15] When we are "on the threshold" of something, we are about to experience something new.

[16] To "go about our lives" simply refers to participating in everyday life.

Unit 2 **ARIANNA HUFFINGTON**

How to Succeed? Get More Sleep

Part 1

My big idea is a very, very small idea that can unlock billions of big ideas that are at the moment dormant inside us. And my little idea that will do that is sleep.

This is a room of type-A women. This is a room of sleep-deprived women. And I **learned the hard way**[1] the value of sleep. Two-and-a-half years ago, I fainted from exhaustion. I hit my head on my desk. I broke my cheekbone. I got five stitches on my right eye. And I began **the journey of rediscovering**[2] the value of sleep. And **in the course of**[3] that, I studied, I met with medical doctors, scientists, and I'm here to tell you that the way to a more productive, more inspired, more joyful life is getting enough sleep.

Part 2

And we women are going to lead the way in this new revolution, this new feminist issue. We are literally going to **sleep our way to the top**,[4] literally.

Because unfortunately for men, sleep deprivation has become a **virility symbol**.[5] I was recently having dinner with a guy who bragged that he had only gotten four hours' sleep the night before. And I felt like saying to him—but I didn't say it—I felt like saying, "You know what? If you had gotten five, this dinner would have been a lot more interesting."

There is now a kind of sleep deprivation **one-upmanship**.[6] Especially here in Washington, if you try to make a **breakfast date**,[7] and you say, "How about eight o'clock?" They're likely to tell you, "Eight o'clock is too late for me, but that's OK, you know, I can get a game of tennis in and do a few **conference calls**[8] and meet you at eight." And they think that means that they are so incredibly busy and productive, but the truth is they're not, because we, at the moment, have had brilliant leaders in business, in finance, in politics, making terrible decisions. So a high I.Q. does not mean that you're a good leader, because the essence of leadership is being able to see the iceberg before it hits the *Titanic*. And we've had far too many icebergs hitting our *Titanics*.

---

[1] To "learn (something) the hard way" means that something negative was experienced before coming to a new realization.

[2] A "journey of rediscovering" (or rediscovery) refers to setting out to relearn something that you once knew, but have forgotten or moved away from.

[3] A synonym for "in the course of" is "during."

[4] To "sleep your way to the top" refers to having sex with superiors at work in order to get promotions. Huffington is making a joke here by using this to explain that sleeping more will contribute to our success at work.

[5] The noun *virility* actually refers to a man's ability to procreate, or his sex drive. However, it is often used as a metaphor to talk about masculinity and power, which is why a "virility symbol" is something that is supposed to make a man seem more masculine and powerful.

[6] "One-upmanship" refers to a competitiveness between people in which one person tries to make themselves sound better than another. For example, if someone says they slept four hours, another person brags that they only slept three.

[7] In this case, a "breakfast date" likely refers to a meeting in the morning over breakfast, not a romantic date.

[8] A "conference call" is a work meeting done over the phone, usually with participants calling in from multiple locations.

In fact, I have a feeling that if Lehman Brothers was Lehman Brothers and Sisters, they might still be around. While all the brothers were busy just being **hyper-connected 24/7,**[9] maybe a sister would have noticed the iceberg, because she would have woken up from a seven-and-a-half- or eight-hour sleep and have been able to **see the big picture.**[10]

So as we are facing all the multiple crises in our world at the moment, what is good for us **on a personal level,**[11] what's going to bring more joy, gratitude, effectiveness in our lives and be the best for our own careers is also what is best for the world. So **I urge you**[12] to shut your eyes and discover the great ideas that lie inside us, to **shut your engines**[13] and discover the power of sleep.

Thank you.

---

[9] The term "hyper-connected 24/7" means to be online and accessible twenty-four hours a day, seven days a week.

[10] When someone can "see the big picture," they have a larger perspective on a given situation or issue.

[11] Something that is "on a personal level" is about our individual lives, experiences, and emotions.

[12] The phrase "I urge you" is a call to action. A speaker uses this phrase to strongly suggest that others follow a suggestion.

[13] Huffington uses the figurative expression "shut your engines" to tell us to go to sleep.

Unit 3 NEIL HARBISSON

I Listen to Color

Part 1

Well, I was born with a rare visual **condition**[1] called achromatopsia, which is total color blindness, so I've never seen color, and I don't know what color looks like, because I come from a grayscale world. To me, the sky is always gray, flowers are always gray, and television is still in black and white.

But, since the age of 21, instead of seeing color, I can hear color. In 2003, I started a project with computer scientist **Adam Montandon**, and the result, with further collaborations with **Peter Kese** from Slovenia and **Matias Lizana**[2] from Barcelona, is this electronic eye. It's a color sensor that detects the **color frequency**[3] in front of me—and sends this frequency to a chip installed at the back of my head, and I hear the color in front of me through the bone, through **bone conduction**.[4] So, for example, if I have, like—this is the sound of purple. For example, this is the sound of grass. This is red, like TED. This is the sound of a dirty sock. Which is like yellow, this one.

So I've been hearing color all the time for eight years, since 2004, so I find it completely normal now to hear color all the time. At the start, though, I had to memorize the names you give for each color, so I had to memorize the notes, but after some time, all this information became a perception. I didn't have to think about the notes. And after some time, this perception became a feeling. I started to have favorite colors, and I started to dream in colors.

So, when I started to dream in color is when I felt that the software and my brain had united, because in my dreams, it was my brain creating electronic sounds. It wasn't the software, so that's when I started to feel like a cyborg. It's when I started to feel that the cybernetic device was no longer a device. It had become a part of my body, an extension of my senses, and after some time, it even became a part of my official image.

This is my passport from 2004. You're not allowed to appear on U.K. passports with electronic equipment, but I insisted to the passport office that what they were seeing was actually a new part of my body, an extension of my brain, and they finally **accepted me**[5] to appear with the passport photo. . . .

Part 2

So I really enjoy creating, like, sound portraits of people. Instead of drawing someone's face, like drawing the shape, I point at them with the eye and I write down the different notes I hear, and then I create sound portraits. Here's some faces. Yeah, Nicole Kidman sounds good. Some people, I would never relate, but they sound similar. Prince Charles has some similarities with Nicole Kidman. They have similar sound of eyes. So you relate people that you wouldn't relate, and you can actually also create concerts by looking at the audience faces. So I connect the eye, and then I play the audience's faces. The good thing about this is, if the concert doesn't sound good, it's their fault. It's not my fault, because . . . And so another thing that happens is that I started having this **secondary effect**[6] that normal sounds started to become color. I heard a **telephone tone**,[7] and it felt green because it sounded just like the color green. The BBC beeps, they sound turquoise, and listening to Mozart became a yellow

---

[1] The term "condition" is often used as a euphemism to describe a medical problem.

[2] Adam Montandon is the computer scientist who worked with Harbisson originally. Peter Kese is the software designer who helped expand the number of colors the Eyeborg could pick up, and Matias Lizana worked on developing the chip for the Eyeborg when he was still a student.

[3] A "color frequency" refers to the rate of vibration per second, measured in terahertz (THz).

[4] When "bone conduction" happens, sound is transmitted to the inner ear via the bones of the skull.

[5] Note that Harbisson's word choice of "accepted me" is not correct English; however, he still communicates clearly that the passport office approved his request.

[6] The expression "secondary effect" refers to a result that wasn't intended or wasn't the main goal, but still has significance. For Harbisson, his main goal was to hear color, but then he started relating colors to every sound he heard, which was also an exciting result.

[7] When Harbisson says "telephone tone," he is likely referring to either the ring of a telephone or the sound heard when the receiver is picked up but a call hasn't been dialed yet.

experience, so I started to paint music and paint people's voices, because people's voices have frequencies that I relate to color.

And here's some music translated into color. For example, Mozart, "Queen of the Night," looks like this. Very yellow and very colorful, because there's many different frequencies. And this is a completely different song. It's **Justin Bieber's**[8] "Baby." It is very pink and very yellow. . . .

So I got to a point when I was able to perceive 360 colors, just like human vision. I was able to differentiate all the degrees of the color wheel. But then, I just thought that this human vision wasn't good enough. There's many, many more colors around us that we cannot perceive, but that **electronic eyes**[9] can perceive. So I decided to continue extending my color senses, and I added infrared and I added ultraviolet to the color-to-sound scale, so now I can hear colors that the human eye cannot perceive. . . .

We should all think that knowledge comes from our senses, so if we extend our senses, we will consequently extend our knowledge. I think life will be much more exciting when we stop creating **applications**[10] for mobile phones and we start creating applications for our own body. I think this will be a big, big change that we'll see during this century. So I do encourage you all to think about which senses you'd like to extend. I would encourage you to become a cyborg. You won't be alone.

Thank you.

---

[8] Justin Bieber is an American pop singer.

[9] Harbisson calls his Eyeborg an "electronic eye."

[10] An "application" or *app* refers to software, often with one specific purpose, used on computers or smartphones.

Unit 4　NIC MARKS

The Happy Planet Index

Part 1

And really, this is what I've done with my **adult life**[1]—is think about how do we measure happiness, how do we measure well-being, how can we do that within environmental limits. And we created, at the organization I work for, the **New Economics Foundation**,[2] something we call the Happy Planet Index, because we think people should be happy and the planet should be happy. Why don't we create a measure of progress that shows that? And what we do, is we say that the ultimate outcome of a nation is how successful is it at creating happy and healthy lives for its citizens. That should be the goal of every nation on the planet. But we have to remember that there's a **fundamental input**[3] to that, and that is how many of the planet's resources we use. We all have one planet. We all have to share it. It is the ultimate scarce resource, the one planet that we share. And economics is very interested in scarcity. When it has a scarce resource that it wants to turn into a **desirable outcome**,[4] it thinks in terms of efficiency. It thinks in terms of **how much bang do we get for our buck**.[5] And this is a measure of how much well-being we get for our planetary resource use. It is an efficiency measure. And probably the easiest way to show you that is to show you this graph.

Running horizontally along the graph is "Ecological footprint," which is a measure of how much resources we use and how much pressure we put on the planet. More is bad. Running vertically upwards, is a measure called "Happy life years." It's about the well-being of nations. It's like a **happiness-adjusted life expectancy**.[6] It's like quality and quantity of life in nations. And the yellow dot there you see, is the global average. Now, there's a huge array of nations around that global average. To the top right of the graph are countries which are doing reasonably well and producing well-being, but they're using a lot of planet to get there. They are the U.S.A., other Western countries going across in those triangles and a few **Gulf states**[7] in there, actually. Conversely, at the bottom left of the graph, are countries that are not producing much well-being — typically, sub-Saharan Africa. In **Hobbesian**[8] terms, life is short and brutish there. Average life expectancy in many of these countries is only 40 years. Malaria, HIV/AIDS are killing a lot of people in these regions of the world.

But now for the good news! There are some countries up there, yellow triangles, that are doing better than global average, that are heading up towards the top left of the graph. This is an aspirational graph. We want to be top left, where

---

[1] A person's "adult life" usually begins after they graduate from school and start working.

[2] For more about the New Economics Foundation, see neweconomics.org.

[3] Marks uses the term "fundamental input" to refer to what each nation uses in its effort to make its people happy.

[4] A "desirable outcome" is a positive result, usually one that has been aimed for.

[5] The expression "bang for your buck" refers to how much value you get for the cost of something. It is often used to talk about the monetary value of something, but Marks is speaking about how much we benefit from using the planet's resources.

[6] A "happiness-adjusted life expectancy" is a figure that takes into account the expected level of happiness in a life, not just the number of years someone is expected to live.

[7] The "Gulf states" are countries in the Middle East on the Persian Gulf.

[8] The term "Hobbesian" refers to Thomas Hobbes (1588–1679), a British philosopher who wrote that man is mostly motivated by selfish reasons.

good lives don't cost the Earth. They're Latin American. The country on its own up at the top is a place I haven't been to. Maybe some of you have: Costa Rica. Costa Rica—average life expectancy is 78-and-a-half years. That is longer than in the U.S.A. They are, according to the latest **Gallup World Poll**,[9] the happiest nation on the planet—than anybody; more than Switzerland and Denmark. They are the happiest place. They are doing that on a quarter of the resources that are used typically in [the] Western world—a quarter of the resources. What's going on there? What's happening in Costa Rica? We can look at some of the data. 99 percent of their electricity comes from renewable resources. Their government is one of the first to commit to be **carbon neutral**[10] by 2021. They abolished the army in 1949—1949. And they invested in social programs—health and education. They have one of the highest literacy rates in Latin America and in the world. And they have that **Latin vibe**,[11] don't they? They have the social connectedness. The challenge is, that possibly—and the thing we might have to think about—is that the future might not be North American, might not be Western European. It might be Latin American. And the challenge, really, is to pull the global average up here. That's what we need to do. And if we're going to do that, we need to pull countries from the bottom, and we need to pull countries from the right of the graph. And then we're starting to create a happy planet. That's one way of looking at it. . . .

Why is it, on the radio news every evening, I hear the FTSE 100, the Dow Jones, the **dollar-pound ratio**[12]—I don't even know which way the dollar-pound should go to be good news. And why do I hear that? Why don't I hear how much energy Britain used yesterday, or America used yesterday? Did we meet our 3 percent annual target on reducing carbon emissions? That's how you create a collective goal. You put it out there into the media and start thinking about it. And we need positive **feedback loops**[13] for increasing well-being. At a government level, they might create national accounts of well-being. At a business level, you might look at the well-being of your employees, which we know is really linked to creativity, which is linked to innovation, and we're going to need a lot of innovation to deal with those environmental issues. At a personal level, we need these **nudges**,[14] too. . . .

Part 2

What are the five things that you should do every day to be happier?

---

[9] The Gallup World Poll is a global survey that collects data and opinions on a range of topics.

[10] Something that is "carbon neutral" sends zero carbon emissions into the atmosphere.

[11] Marks uses the term "that Latin vibe" to describe the lively, warm atmosphere associated with Latin nations and its' people.

[12] The "dollar-pound ratio" refers to the strength of the British pound versus the U.S. dollar.

[13] A "feedback loop" is an economic term that refers to a situation where the product or output is used again as input.

[14] A "nudge" is a gentle push. Marks is using it here as a synonym for "reminder."

We did a project for the **Government Office of Science**[15] a couple of years ago, a big program called the Foresight program—lots and lots of people—involved lots of experts—everything evidence-based—a huge tome. But a piece of work we did was on: What five positive actions can you do to improve well-being in your life? And the point of these is they are not quite the secrets of happiness, but they are things that I think happiness will flow out the side from. And the first of these is to connect, is that your social relationships are the most important cornerstones of your life. Do you invest the time with your loved ones that you could do, and energy? Keep building them. The second one is be active. Fastest way out of a bad mood: Step outside, go for a walk, turn the radio on and dance. Being active is great for our positive mood. The third one is take notice. How aware are you of things going on around the world, the seasons changing, people around you? Do you notice what's **bubbling up**[16] for you and trying to emerge? Based on a lot of evidence for **mindfulness**,[17] cognitive behavioral therapy, very strong for our well-being. The fourth is keep learning and keep is important—learning throughout the whole life course. Older people who keep learning and are curious, they have much better health outcomes than those who start to close down. But it doesn't have to be formal learning; it's not knowledge-based. It's more curiosity. It can be learning to cook a new dish, picking up an instrument you forgot as a child. Keep learning. And the final one is that most anti-economic of activities, but give. Our generosity, our altruism, our compassion, are all **hardwired**[18] to the reward mechanism in our brain. We feel good if we give. You can do an experiment where you give two groups of people a hundred dollars in the morning. You tell one of them to spend it on themselves and one on other people. You measure their happiness at the end of the day, that those that have gone and spent on other people are much happier than those that spent it on themselves.

And these five ways, which we put onto these handy postcards, I would say, **don't have to cost the Earth.**[19] They don't have any carbon content. They don't need a lot of material goods to be satisfied. And so I think it's really quite feasible that happiness does not cost the Earth. . . .

---

[15] The Government Offices of Science is a U.K. organization whose role is to advise the government by providing up-to-date science reports to inform government policies.

[16] Something that is "bubbling up" is coming to the surface. Marks is using it to refer to ideas, thoughts, and awareness.

[17] "Mindfulness" refers to a state of being connected with a present situation both mentally and emotionally by giving it your full attention.

[18] Marks uses "hardwired" to point out that something is physiologically a part of our makeup.

[19] The expression "don't have to cost the Earth," which Marks uses twice at the end of his speech, is used to explain that something doesn't have to be expensive. However, Marks is also using this as a pun, to point out that to be happy, one does not have to use up all of the Earth's resources.

The Power of Time Off

Part 1

I run a design studio in New York. Every seven years, I close it for one year to pursue some **little experiments**,[1] things that are always difficult to accomplish during the regular working year. In that year, we are not available for any of our clients. We are totally closed. And as you can imagine, it is a lovely and very energetic time.

I originally had opened the studio in New York to combine my two loves, music and design. And we created videos and packaging for many musicians that you know, and for even more that you've never heard of. As I realized, just like with many, many things in my life that I actually love, I adapt to it. And I get, over time, bored by them. And for sure, in our case, our work started to look the same. You see here a glass eye in a **die cut**[2] of a book. Quite the similar idea, then, a perfume packaged in a book, in a die cut. So I decided to close it down for one year.

Also is the knowledge that right now we spend about in the first 25 years of our lives learning, then there is another 40 years that's really reserved for working. And then **tacked on at the end of**[3] it are about 15 years for retirement.

And I thought it might be helpful to basically cut off five of those retirement years and intersperse them in between those working years. That's clearly enjoyable for myself. But probably even more important is that the work that comes out of these years flows back into the company and into society at large, rather than just benefiting a grandchild or two. There is a fellow **TEDster**[4] who spoke two years ago, Jonathan Haidt, who defined his work into three different levels. And they **rang very true**[5] for me. I can see my work as a job. I do it for money. I likely already look forward to the weekend on Thursdays. And I probably will need a hobby as a **leveling mechanism**.[6] In a career, I'm definitely more engaged. But at the same time, there will be periods when I think is all that really hard work really worth my while? While in the third one, in the calling, very much likely I would do it also if I wouldn't be financially compensated for it. . . .

Part 2

If I look at my cycle, seven years, one-year sabbatical, it's 12.5 percent of my time. And if I look at companies that are actually more successful than mine, 3M since the 1930s is giving all their engineers 15 percent to pursue whatever

---

[1] Sagmeister uses the term "little experiments" to refer to creative pursuits or non-work-related projects.

[2] A "die cut" is the cutting of paper or card using machines with sharp, steel knives.

[3] Something that is "tacked on the end" or "tacked on at the end" is added after something else is finished, usually without careful thought. A *tack* is a type of short nail with a flat head.

[4] The term "TEDster" refers to an individual who has given a TED Talk.

[5] When something you hear or see "rings true" for you, it feels relevant and accurate for you.

[6] A "leveling mechanism" is something that creates a flat surface. In this case, Marks means that he needs a hobby to have a better balance between work and life.

they want. There [are] some good successes. **Scotch tape**[7] came out of this program, as well as Art Fry developed **sticky notes**[8] from during his personal time for 3M. Google, of course, very famously gives 20 percent for their software engineers to pursue their own personal projects. . . .

When I had the idea of doing one, the process was I made the decision and I put it into my **daily planner book**.[9] And then I told as many, many people as I possibly could about it so that there was no way that I could **chicken out**[10] later on. In the beginning, on the first sabbatical, it was **rather disastrous**.[11] I had thought that I should do this without any plan, that this vacuum of time somehow would be wonderful and enticing for idea generation. It was not. I just, without a plan, I just reacted to little requests, not work requests—those I all said no to—but other little requests. Sending mail to Japanese design magazines and things like that. So I became my own **intern**.[12]

And I very quickly made a list of the things that I was interested in, put them in a hierarchy, divided them into chunks of time, and then made a plan, very much like in **grade school**.[13] What does it say here? Monday, 8 to 9: story writing; 9 to 10: future thinking. Was not very successful. And so on and so forth. And that actually, specifically as a starting point of the first sabbatical, worked really well for me. What came out of it? I really got close to design again. I had fun. Financially, seen over the long term, it was actually successful. Because of the improved quality, we could ask for higher prices. And probably most importantly, basically everything we've done in the seven years following the first sabbatical came out of thinking of that one single year.

And I'll show you a couple of projects that came out of the seven years following that sabbatical. . . . This is a whole wall of bananas at different ripenesses on the opening day in this gallery in New York. It says, "Self-confidence produces fine

---

[7] "Scotch tape" is a popular cellophane tape sold by 3M.

[8] "Sticky notes," also known as Post-its, are small pieces of paper with adhesive on the back of them.

[9] A "daily planner book" refers to a book with a calendar in which a person writes his or her daily schedule.

[10] To "chicken out" means to decide not to do something because of fear.

[11] Sagmeister uses the term "rather disastrous" to mean it did not go well at all.

[12] An "intern" is a young staff member, often a student, who works for no pay or a very low salary in order to gain work experience.

[13] "Grade school" refers to elementary or primary school.

results." This is after a week. After two weeks, three weeks, four weeks, five weeks. And you see the self-confidence almost comes back, but not quite. These are some pictures visitors sent to me. And then the city of Amsterdam gave us a plaza and asked us to do something. We used the stone plates as a grid for our little piece. We got 250,000 coins from the central bank, at different darknesses. So we got brand-new ones, shiny ones, medium ones, and very old, dark ones. And with the help of 100 volunteers, over a week, created this fairly floral typography that spelled, "Obsessions make my life worse and my work better." . . .

We are also working on the start of a bigger project in Bali. It's a movie about happiness. And here we asked some nearby pigs to do the titles for us. They weren't quite **slick**[14] enough. So we asked the goose to do it again, and hoped she would do somehow, a more elegant or pretty job. And I think she overdid it. Just a bit too ornamental. And my studio is very close to the monkey forest. And the monkeys in that monkey forest looked, actually, fairly happy. So we asked those guys to do it again. They did a fine job, but had a couple of **readability problems**.[15] So of course whatever you don't really do yourself doesn't really get done properly. That film we'll be working on for the next two years. . . .

Thank you.

---

[14] Sagmeister says that the pigs in his project weren't quite "slick" enough to explain that the outcome wasn't as nice as he had hoped.

[15] Sagmeister continues to joke about working with the animals by describing the monkeys as having "readability problems."

Unit 6   JOHN McWHORTER

Txtng Is Killing Language. JK!!!

Part 1

What texting is, despite the fact that it involves the **brute mechanics[1]** of something that we call writing, is **fingered speech**.[2] That's what texting is. Now we can write the way we talk. And it's a very interesting thing, but nevertheless, easy to think that still it represents some sort of decline. We see this general bagginess of the structure, the lack of concern with rules and the way that we're used to **learning on the blackboard**,[3] and so we think that something has **gone wrong**.[4] It's a very natural sense.

But **the fact of the matter is that[5]** what is going on is a kind of emergent complexity. That's what we're seeing in this fingered speech. And in order to understand it, what we want to see is the way, in this new kind of language, there is new structure coming up.

And so, for example, there is in texting a convention, which is LOL. Now LOL, we generally think of as meaning "laughing out loud." And of course, theoretically, it does, and if you look at older texts, then people used it to actually indicate laughing out loud. But if you text now, or if you are someone who is aware of the **substrate[6]** of texting the way it's become, you'll notice that LOL does not mean laughing out loud anymore. It's evolved into something that is much subtler.

This is an actual text that was done by a **non-male person of about 20 years old[7]** not too long ago. "I love the font you're using, btw." Julie: "lol thanks gmail is being slow right now." Now if you think about it, that's not funny. No one's laughing. And yet, there it is, so you assume there's been some kind of **hiccup**.[8] Then Susan says "lol, I know," again more guffawing than we're used to when you're talking about these inconveniences. So Julie says, "I just sent you an email." Susan: "lol, I see it." Very funny people, if that's what LOL means. This Julie says, "So what's up?" Susan: "lol, I have to write a 10 page paper."

She's not amused. Let's think about it. LOL is being used in a very particular way. It's a marker of empathy. It's a marker of accommodation. We linguists call things like that pragmatic particles. Any spoken language that's used by real people has them. If you happen to speak Japanese, think about that little word *ne* that you use at the end of a lot of sentences. If you listen to the way **black youth[9]** today speak, think about the use of the word *yo*. Whole dissertations could be written about it, and probably are being written about it. A pragmatic

---

[1] By using the expression "brute mechanics," McWhorter is emphasizing that texting is a physical task (that resembles writing).

[2] The term "fingered speech" is a clear description of what texting is: speaking by writing with your fingers. He explains this in the sentence that follows when he says that with texting, "we can write the way we talk."

[3] McWhorter uses "learning on the blackboard" as a figurative way to refer to formal education.

[4] When something "goes wrong," a problem is experienced.

[5] The expression "the fact of the matter is that" is a synonym for "in fact."

[6] A "substrate" is a layer, often of something that is growing, and in this case McWhorter uses the term to infer that the language of texting is evolving.

[7] Note that instead of saying "a teenage girl," McWhorter uses the more entertaining expression of "a non-male person of about 20 years old."

[8] The word "hiccup" is used as a euphemism for a small mistake.

[9] When he says "black youth today," McWhorter is mostly referring to black youth in the U.S.

particle, that's what LOL has gradually become. It's a way of using the language between actual people. . . .

Part 2

Another example is *slash*. Now, we can use slash in the way that we're used to, along the lines of, "We're going to have a party-slash-networking session." That's kind of like what we're at. *Slash* is used in a very different way in texting among young people today. It's used to change the **scene**.[10] So for example, this Sally person says, "So I need to find people to **chill**[11] with" and Jake says, "Haha"—you could write a dissertation about "Haha" too, but we don't have time for that—"Haha so you're going by yourself? Why?" Sally: "For this summer program at NYU." Jake: "Haha. Slash I'm watching this video with suns players trying to shoot with one eye."

The slash is interesting. I don't really even know what Jake is talking about after that, but you notice that he's changing the topic. Now that seems kind of mundane, but think about how in real life, if we're having a conversation and we want to change the topic, there are ways of doing it gracefully. You don't just **zip**[12] right into it. You'll pat your thighs and look wistfully off into the distance, or you'll say something like, "Hmm, makes you think"—when it really didn't, but what you're really—what you're really trying to do is change the topic. You can't do that while you're texting, and so ways are developing of doing it within this medium. All spoken languages have what a linguist calls a new information marker—or two, or three. Texting has developed one from this *slash*. . . .

And so, the way I'm thinking of texting these days is that what we're seeing is a whole new way of writing that young people are developing, which they're using alongside their ordinary writing skills, and that means that they're able to do two things. Increasing evidence is that being bilingual is cognitively beneficial. That's also true of being bidialectal. That's certainly true of being bidialectal in terms of your writing. And so texting actually is evidence of **a balancing act**[13] that young people are using today, not consciously, of course, but it's an expansion of their linguistic repertoire . . .

---

[10] A synonym for "scene" in this sentence is "topic."

[11] Sally is using the slang word "chill" to mean "hang out" or "spend time with."

[12] The verb "zip" here is used to describe being overly direct in an action.

[13] The expression "a balancing act" refers to a situation when two different things must be done simultaneously.

Unit 7　**CHIMAMANDA NGOZI ADICHIE**

The Danger of a Single Story

Part 1

I'm a storyteller. And I would like to tell you a few personal stories about what I like to call "the danger of the single story." I grew up on a university campus in eastern Nigeria. My mother says that I started reading at the age of two, although I think four is probably close to the truth. So I was an early reader, and what I read were British and American children's books.

I was also an early writer, and when I began to write, at about the age of seven, stories in pencil with crayon illustrations that **my poor mother[1]** was obligated to read, I wrote exactly the kinds of stories I was reading: All my characters were white and blue-eyed, they played in the snow, they ate apples, and they talked a lot about the weather, how **lovely[2]** it was that the sun had come out. Now, this despite the fact that I lived in Nigeria. I had never been outside Nigeria. We didn't have snow, we ate mangoes, and we never talked about the weather, because there was no need to.

My characters also drank a lot of **ginger beer[3]** because the characters in the British books I read drank ginger beer. Never mind that I had no idea what ginger beer was. And for many years afterwards, I would have a desperate desire to taste ginger beer. But that is another story.

What this demonstrates, I think, is how impressionable and vulnerable we are in the face of a story, particularly as children. Because all I had read were books in which characters were foreign, I had become convinced that books by their very nature had to have foreigners in them and had to be about things with which I could not personally identify. Now, things changed when I discovered African books. There weren't many of them available, and they weren't quite as easy to find as the foreign books.

But because of writers like Chinua Achebe and Camara Laye, I went through a mental shift in my perception of literature. I realized that people like me, girls with skin the color of

---

[1] The adjective "poor" is often used to offer someone sympathy in a situation. Adichie is partly making fun of herself here as she sympathizes with her mother who had to read all her young stories.

[2] The adjective "lovely" describes something pleasant. It is more popularly used in British English than American English.

[3] The drink "ginger beer" is usually a non-alcoholic, carbonated, sweet drink. There are also alcoholic versions. In the U.S., a somewhat similar drink is called "ginger ale."

chocolate, whose **kinky hair could not form ponytails**,[4] could also exist in literature. I started to write about things I recognized.

Now, I loved those American and British books I read. They stirred my imagination. They opened up new worlds for me. But the **unintended consequence**[5] was that I did not know that people like me could exist in literature. So what the discovery of African writers did for me was this: It saved me from having a single story of what books are.

Part 2

I come from a conventional, middle-class Nigerian family. My father was a professor. My mother was an administrator. And so we had, as was the norm, live-in **domestic help**,[6] who would often come from nearby rural villages. So the year I turned eight, we got a new **houseboy**.[7] His name was Fide. The only thing my mother told us about him was that his family was very poor. My mother sent yams and rice, and our old clothes, to his family. And when I didn't finish my dinner, my mother would say, "Finish your food! Don't you know? People like Fide's family have nothing." So I felt enormous pity for Fide's family.

Then one Saturday we went to his village to visit, and his mother showed us a beautifully patterned basket made of dyed raffia that his brother had made. I was startled. It had not occurred to me that anybody in his family could actually make something. All I had heard about them was how poor they were, so that it had become impossible for me to see them as anything else but poor. Their poverty was my single story of them.

Years later, I thought about this when I left Nigeria to go to university in the United States. I was 19. My American roommate was shocked by me. She asked where I had learned to speak English so well, and was confused when I said that Nigeria happened to have English as its official language. She asked if she could listen to what she called my "tribal music," and was consequently very disappointed when I produced my tape of Mariah Carey. She assumed that I did not know how to use a stove.

What struck me was this: She had felt sorry for me even before she saw me. Her default position toward me, as an African, was a kind of patronizing, well-meaning pity. My roommate had a single story of Africa: **a single story of catastrophe**.[8] In this single story, there was no possibility

---

[4] The adjective "kinky" is commonly used to describe black or African hair. By pointing out that her hair cannot go in a "ponytail," Adichie is illustrating again how different she was from the white protagonists in the stories she read.

[5] An "unintended consequence" is not a primary one, but secondary.

[6 & 7] Adichie uses both the words "domestic help" and "houseboy" to refer to someone who lives in her home to help with cleaning, cooking, and other chores. The former is the more generic, accepted term to describe such a job. The term "houseboy" was likely a common colloquialism when Adichie was young.

[8] The "single story of catastrophe" that she describes refers to the problems of poverty, illness, and famine that are often associated with Africa.

of Africans being similar to her in any way, no possibility of feelings more complex than pity, no possibility of a connection as human equals. . . .

But I must quickly add that I, too, am just as guilty in the question of the single story. A few years ago, I visited Mexico from the U.S. The **political climate**[9] in the U.S. at the time was tense, and there were debates going on about immigration. And, as often happens in America, immigration became synonymous with Mexicans. There were endless stories of Mexicans as people who were **fleecing**[10] the healthcare system, sneaking across the border, being arrested at the border, that sort of thing.

I remember walking around on my first day in Guadalajara, watching the people going to work, rolling up tortillas in the marketplace, smoking, laughing. I remember first feeling slight surprise. And then I was overwhelmed with shame. I realized that I had been so immersed in the media coverage of Mexicans that they had become one thing in my mind: the abject immigrant. I had bought into the single story of Mexicans, and I could not have been more ashamed of myself. So that is how to create a single story, show a people as one thing, as only one thing, over and over again, and that is what they become.

. . . But to insist on only these negative stories is to **flatten my experience**[11] and to overlook the many other stories that formed me. The single story creates stereotypes, and the problem with stereotypes is not that they are untrue, but that they are incomplete. They make one story become the only story. . . . I've always felt that it is impossible to engage properly with a place or a person without engaging with all of the stories of that place and that person. The consequence of the single story is this: It robs people of dignity. It makes our recognition of our equal humanity difficult. It emphasizes how we are different rather than how we are similar.

. . . I teach writing workshops in Lagos every summer, and it is amazing to me how many people apply, how many people are eager to write, to tell stories. My Nigerian publisher and I have just started a non-profit called **Farafina**[12] Trust, and we have big dreams of building libraries and refurbishing libraries that already exist and providing books for state schools that don't have anything in their libraries, and also of organizing lots and lots of workshops, in reading and writing, for all the people who are eager to tell our many stories. Stories matter. Many stories matter. Stories have been used to dispossess and to malign, but stories can also be used to empower and to humanize. Stories can break the dignity of a people, but stories can also repair that broken dignity. . . .

---

[9] The term "political climate" is used to describe the populace's general attitude, and surrounding tensions, in regards to a certain political topic or social issue at the time.

[10] To "fleece" someone means to dishonestly take money from them.

[11] Adiche is likely using the word "flatten" here to describe how stereotypes make our experiences one-dimensional.

[12] Farafina's website is farafinatrust.org.

Unit 8 SUSAN CAIN

The Power of Introverts

Part 1

A third to a half of the population are introverts—a third to a half. So that's one out of every two or three people you know. So even if you're an extrovert yourself, I'm talking about your co-workers and your spouses and your children and the person sitting right next to you right now—all of them **subject to this bias**[1] that is pretty deep and real in our society. We all **internalize**[2] it from a very early age without even having a language for what we're doing. . . .

But now, here's where the bias comes in. Our most important institutions, our schools and our workplaces, they are designed mostly for extroverts and for extroverts' need for lots of stimulation. And also, we're living through this belief system, we have a belief system right now that I call the new groupthink, which holds that all creativity and all productivity comes from a very oddly gregarious place.

So if you picture the typical classroom nowadays: When I was going to school, we sat in rows. We sat in rows of desks like this, and we did most of our work pretty autonomously. But nowadays, your typical classroom has **pods of desks**[3]—four or five or six or seven kids all facing each other. And kids are working in countless group assignments. Even in subjects like math and creative writing, which you would think would depend on solo flights of thought, kids are now expected to act as **committee members**.[4] And for the kids who prefer to go off by themselves or just to work alone, those kids are seen as **outliers**[5] often or, worse, as problem cases. And the vast majority of teachers reports believing that the ideal student is an extrovert as opposed to an introvert, even though introverts actually get better grades and are more knowledgeable, according to research.

OK, same thing is true in our workplaces. We now, most of us, work in **open-plan offices**,[6] without walls, where we are subject to the constant noise and gaze of our co-workers. And when it comes to leadership, introverts are routinely passed over for leadership positions, even though introverts tend to be very careful, much less likely to take **outsized risks**[7]—which is something we might all favor nowadays. And interesting research by **Adam Grant**[8] at the Wharton School has found that introverted leaders often deliver better outcomes than extroverts do, because when they are managing proactive employees, they're much more likely to let those employees run with their ideas, whereas an extrovert can, quite unwittingly, get so excited about things that they're **putting their own stamp on**[9] things, and other people's ideas might not as easily then bubble up to the surface. . . .

Part 2

Now if all this is true, then why are we **getting it so wrong**?[10] Why are we setting up our schools this way and our workplaces? And why are we making these introverts feel so guilty about wanting to just go off by themselves some of the time? One answer lies deep in our cultural history. Western societies, and in particular the U.S., have always favored the man of action over the man of contemplation and "man" of contemplation. But in **America's early days**,[11] we lived

---

[1] When someone is "subject to bias," they are treated unfairly due to others' discriminatory beliefs.

[2] When we "internalize" a belief, we begin to unconsciously think it's the truth, usually because we have heard it often (not because we agree with it).

[3] A classroom with "pods of desks" is usually set up so that three or four desks are turned into each other, which means students face each other as they work. This classroom layout is supposed to encourage group work.

[4] Instead of saying "teamwork," Cain describes it as "committee members." We can infer from her language choice that she sees this option as not ideal. This is especially clear in noting that she describes working individually with positive language: "solo flights of thought."

[5] An "outlier" is an individual alienated from the group. It is not a positive term.

[6] An "open-plan office" is organized so that all desks are visible to everyone. There are usually no walls or doors. Note that students saw a picture of an open-plan office in Lesson A.

[7] A synonym for "outsized" is "large" or "oversized."

[8] Adam Grant is a business professor and social science writer. He is the author of *Give and Take*.

[9] When you "put your own stamp on something," you make it or claim it as yours by adding your ideas to it somehow.

[10] Note that "bubble up," meaning "to emerge," was also used by TED speaker Nic Marks in Unit 4.

[11] "America's early days" refers to when the nation was founded in the 1700s.

in what historians call a culture of character, where we still, at that point, valued people for their inner selves and their moral rectitude. And if you look at the **self-help books**[12] from this era, they all had titles with things like "Character, the Grandest Thing in the World." And they featured role models like **Abraham Lincoln**[13] who was praised for being modest and unassuming. **Ralph Waldo Emerson**[14] called him "A man who does not offend by superiority."

But then we hit the 20th century and we entered a new culture that historians call the culture of personality. What happened is we had evolved from an agricultural economy to a world of big business. And so suddenly people are moving from small towns to the cities. And instead of working alongside people they've known all their lives, now they are having to prove themselves in a crowd of strangers. So, quite understandably, qualities like magnetism and charisma suddenly come to seem really important. And sure enough, the self-help books change to meet these new needs and they start to have names like *How to Win Friends and Influence People*. And they feature as their role models really great salesmen. So that's the world we're living in today. That's our cultural inheritance.

Now none of this is to say that social skills are unimportant, and I'm also not calling for the abolishing of teamwork at all. The same religions who send their sages off to lonely mountaintops also teach us love and trust. And the problems that we are facing today in fields like science and in economics are so vast and so complex that we are going to need **armies of**[15] people coming together to solve them working together. But I am saying that the more freedom that we give introverts to be themselves, the more likely that they are to come up with their own unique solutions to these problems. . . .

So I just published a book about introversion, and it took me about seven years to write. And for me, that seven years was like total bliss, because I was reading, I was writing, I was thinking, I was researching. It was my version of my grandfather's hours a day alone in his library. But now all of a sudden my job is very different, and my job is to be out here talking about it, talking about introversion. And that's a lot harder for me, because as honored as I am to be here with all of you right now, this is not my natural milieu.

So I prepared for moments like these as best I could. I spent the last year practicing public speaking every chance I could get. And I call this my **"year of speaking dangerously."**[16] And that actually helped a lot. But I'll tell you, what helps even more is my sense, my belief, my hope that when it comes to our attitudes to introversion and to quiet and to solitude, we truly are poised on the brink of dramatic change. . . So I wish you the best of all possible journeys and the courage to speak softly.

Thank you very much.

---

[12] A "self-help book" refers to a book written on a topic that encourages people to improve themselves.

[13] Abraham Lincoln became the 16th President of the United States in 1861. He was president during the Civil War that lead to the abolishment of slavery.

[14] Ralph Waldo Emerson was a writer and speaker in the U.S. in the 1800s. He is best known for being a leader of the Transcendentalist movement. Transcendentalists believed that individuals have to be free to develop independently in order to be good members of society.

[15] The term "armies of" is used when a large number of people or things are needed to get something done.

[16] When Cain says that it is her "year of speaking dangerously," she is making a humorous comment by referencing a popular novel and movie titled *The Year of Living Dangerously*.

The Gentle Genius of Bonobos

Part 1

There are many people who think that the animal world is **hardwired**[1] and that there's something very, very special about man. Maybe it's his ability to have **causal thought**.[2] Maybe it's something special in his brain that allows him to have language. Maybe it's something special in his brain that allows him to make tools or have mathematics . . .

So what I want to do now is introduce you to a species called the bonobo. This is Kanzi. He's a bonobo. Right now, he's in a forest in Georgia. His mother originally came from a forest in Africa. And she came to us when she was just at puberty, about six or seven years of age. . . .

This is Kanzi and I, in the forest. None of the things you will see in this particular video are trained. None of them are tricks. They all happened to be captured on film spontaneously, by NHK of Japan. We have eight bonobos.

Savage-Rumbaugh (video): Look at all this stuff that's here for our campfire. S-R: An entire family at our research center. S-R (video): You going to help get some sticks? Good. We need more sticks, too. I have a lighter in my pocket if you need one. That's a wasps' nest. You can get it out. I hope I have a lighter. You can use the lighter to start the fire. S-R: So Kanzi is very interested in fire. He doesn't do it yet without a lighter, but I think if he saw someone do it, he might be able to do—make a fire without a lighter. He's learning about how to keep a fire going. He's learning the uses for a fire, just by watching what we do with fire. . . . This is his sister. This is her first time to try to drive a golf cart. S-R (video): Good-bye. S-R: She's **got** the pedals **down**,[3] but not the wheel. She switches from reverse to forward and she holds onto the wheel, rather than turns it. Like us, she knows that that individual in the mirror is her. Narrator: By raising bonobos in a culture that is both bonobo and human, and documenting their development across two decades, scientists are exploring how cultural forces may have operated during human evolution. His name is Nyota. It means "star" in Swahili. Panbanisha is trying to give Nyota a haircut with a pair of scissors. In the wild, the parent bonobo is known to **groom**[4] its offspring. Here Panbanisha uses scissors, instead of her hands, to groom Nyota. Very impressive. Subtle maneuvering of the hands

---

[1] Note that the term "hardwired" was also used by TED speaker Nic Marks. In this case, Savage-Rumbaugh is referring to our biological make-up.

[2] "Causal thought" refers to recognizing cause-and-effect relationships between events and using this to problem-solve and understand your surroundings.

[3] When someone has "got something down," it means they understand. Savage-Rumbaugh is saying that Kanzi's sister has figured out how the pedals work, just not the steering wheel.

[4] The verb "groom" is more commonly used to talk about animals than humans. With animals, it means to brush or clean hair or fur. With humans, it involves tidying your appearance, such as fixing your hair or putting on makeup.

is required to perform delicate tasks like this. Nyota tries to imitate Panbanisha by using the scissors himself. Realizing that Nyota might get hurt, Panbanisha, like any human mother, carefully tugs to get the scissors back. . . . He can now cut through tough animal **hide**.[5] S-R Kanzi's learned to make stone tools. Narr: Kanzi now makes his tools, just as our ancestors may have made them, two-and-a-half million years ago—by holding the rocks in both hands, to strike one against the other. He has learned that by using both hands and aiming his glancing blows, he can make much larger, sharper **flakes**.[6] Kanzi chooses a flake he thinks is sharp enough. The tough hide is difficult to cut, even with a knife. The rock that Kanzi is using is extremely hard and ideal for stone tool-making, but difficult to handle, requiring great skill. Kanzi's rock is from Gona, Ethiopia, and is identical to that used by our African ancestors two-and-a-half million years ago. These are the rocks Kanzi used and these are the flakes he made. The flat, sharp edges are like knife blades. Compare them to the tools our ancestors used; they **bear a striking resemblance**[7] to Kanzi's.

Part 2

S-R: These are her symbols on her keyboard. They speak when she touches them. Narr: Panbanisha is communicating to Dr. Sue where she wants to go. **"A-frame"**[8] represents a hut in the woods. Compare the chalk writing with the **lexigram**[9] on the keyboard. Panbanisha began writing the lexigrams on the forest floor. S-R (video): Very nice. Beautiful, Panbanisha. S-R: At first we didn't really realize what she was doing, until we stood back and looked at it and rotated it. Narr: This lexigram also refers to a place in the woods. The curved line is very similar to the lexigram. The next symbol Panbanisha writes represents "collar." It indicates the collar Panbanisha must wear when she goes out. S-R: That's an **institutional requirement**.[10] Narr: This symbol is not as clear as the others, but one can see Panbanisha is trying to produce a curved line and several straight lines. Researchers began to record what Panbanisha said, by writing lexigrams on the floor with chalk. Panbanisha watched. Soon she began to write as well. The bonobo's abilities have stunned scientists around the world. How did they develop?

---

[5] A "hide" is animal skin that has been made into leather.

[6] The noun "flake" here is an archeological term that refers to a small, sharp piece of stone that has been intentionally broken off to be used as a tool.

[7] Something that "bears a striking resemblance" to something else looks almost exactly the same.

[8] An "A-frame" describes the triangle shape of a simply constructed building.

[9] A "lexigram" is a symbol that represents a specific word.

[10] When Savage-Rumbaugh says "institutional requirement," she means that it's a rule in their research facility. Anytime a bonobo goes outside, the ape must wear a collar.

S-R (video): We found that the most important thing for permitting bonobos to acquire language is not to teach them. It's simply to use language around them, because the driving force in language acquisition is to understand what others, that are important to you, are saying to you. Once you have that capacity, the ability to produce language comes rather naturally and rather freely. So we want to create an environment in which bonobos, like all of the individuals with whom they are interacting—we want to create an environment in which they have fun, and an environment in which the others are meaningful individuals for them. Narr: This environment brings out unexpected potential in Kanzi and Panbanisha. . . .

Researcher (video): OK, now get the **monsters**.[11] Get them. Take the cherries, too. Now watch out, stay away from them now. Now you can chase them again. Time to chase them. Now you have to stay away. Get away. Run away. Run. Now we can chase them again. Go get them. Oh, no! Good, Kanzi. Very good. Thank you so much. . . . S-R: So we have a bi-species environment; we call it a "panhomoculture." We're learning how to become like them. We're learning how to communicate with them, in really high-pitched tones. We're learning that they probably have a language in the wild. And they're learning to become like us. Because we believe that it's not biology; it's culture. So we're sharing tools and technology and language with another species.

Thank you.

---

[11] The word "monsters" is used to refer to the creatures in the video game that the bonobo is playing in the video. The video game, called Pac-Man, was popular during the 1980s.

Unit 10 **CHRIS HADFIELD**

What I Learned from Going Blind in Space

Part 1

What's the scariest thing you've ever done? Or another way to say it is, what's the most dangerous thing that you've ever done? And why did you do it? I know what the most dangerous thing is that I've ever done because NASA does the math. You look back to the first five shuttle launches, the odds of a catastrophic event during the first five shuttle launches was one in nine. And even when I first flew in the shuttle back in 1995, 74 shuttle flight, the **odds**[1] were still now that we look back about 1 in 38 or so—1 in 35, one in 40. Not great odds, so it's a really interesting day when you wake up at the **Kennedy Space Center**[2] and you're going to go to space that day because you realize by the end of the day you're either going to be floating effortlessly, gloriously in space, or you'll be dead. . . .

Announcer: 12, 11, 10, 9, 8, 7, 6—start, 2, 1, booster ignition, and liftoff of the space shuttle Discovery, returning to the space station, paving the way . . .

Hadfield: It is incredibly powerful to be on board one of these things. You are **in the grip of**[3] something that is vastly more powerful than yourself. It's shaking you so hard, you can't focus on the instruments in front of you. It's like you're in the jaws of some enormous dog and there's a foot in the small of your back pushing you into space, accelerating wildly straight up, shouldering your way through the air, and you're in a very complex place—paying attention, watching the vehicle go through each one of its **wickets**[4] with a steadily increasing smile on your face. After two minutes, those solid rockets explode off and then you just have the liquid engines, the hydrogen and oxygen, and it's as if **you're in a dragster with your foot to the floor**[5] and accelerating like you've never accelerated. You get lighter and lighter, the force gets on us heavier and heavier. It feels like someone's pouring cement on you or something. Until finally, after about eight minutes and 40 seconds or so, we are finally at exactly the right altitude, exactly the right speed, the right direction, the engine shut off, and we're weightless. And we're alive.

It's an amazing experience. But why would we take that risk? Why would you do something that dangerous? In my case, the answer is fairly straightforward. I was inspired as a youngster that this is what I wanted to do. I watched the first people walk on the moon and to me, it was just an obvious thing—I want to somehow turn myself into that. But the real question is, how do you deal with the danger of it and the fear that comes from it? How do you deal with fear versus danger?

And having the goal in mind, thinking about where it might lead, directed me to a life of looking at all of the small details

---

[1] The plural noun "odds" describes a ratio of likelihood that something will happen. The term is commonly used in gambling or betting.

[2] The Kennedy Space Center, in Florida, is where NASA's shuttles launch from.

[3] To be "in the grip of" something describes a state of not being in control of your actions. The "something" has more power than you do in the situation.

[4] The noun "wicket" here is used to describe the checkpoints or stages along the way that the shuttle must go through in order to safely make it to space.

[5] A "dragster" refers to a car made for racing, and to have your "foot to the floor" means that you are accelerating that car as fast as it can go.

to allow this to become possible, to be able to launch and go help build a space station where you are on board a million-pound creation that's going around the world at five miles a second, eight kilometers a second, around the world 16 times a day, with **experiments on board that are teaching us what the substance of the universe is made of**[6] and running 200 experiments inside. But maybe even more importantly, allowing us to see the world in a way that is impossible through any other means, to be able to look down and have—if your jaw could drop, it would—the jaw-dropping gorgeousness of the turning orb like a self-propelled art gallery of fantastic, constantly changing beauty that is the world itself. And you see, because of the speed, a sunrise or a sunset every 45 minutes for half a year. And the most magnificent part of all that is to go outside on a spacewalk.

You are in a one-person spaceship that is your spacesuit, and you're going through space with the world. It's an entirely different perspective, you're not looking up at the universe, you and the Earth are going through the universe together. And you're holding on with one hand, looking at the world turn beside you. It's roaring silently with color and texture as it pours by just mesmerizingly next to you. And if you can tear your eyes away from that and you look under your arm down at the rest of everything, it's unfathomable blackness, with a texture you feel like you could stick your hand into. And you are holding on with one hand, one link to the other seven billion people.

Part 2

And I was outside on my first spacewalk when my left eye went blind, and I didn't know why. Suddenly my left eye **slammed shut**[7] in great pain and I couldn't figure out why my eye wasn't working. I was thinking, what do I do next? I thought, well, maybe that's why we have two eyes, so I kept working. But unfortunately, without gravity, tears don't fall. So you just get a bigger and bigger ball of whatever that is mixed with your tears on your eye until eventually, the ball becomes so big that the surface tension takes it across the bridge of your nose like a tiny little waterfall and goes **"goosh"**[8] into your other eye, and now I was completely blind outside the spaceship. . . .

If you're outside on a spacewalk and you're blinded, your natural reaction would be to panic, I think. It would make you nervous and worried. But we had considered **all the venom, and we had practiced with a whole variety of different spider webs.**[9] We knew everything there is to know about the spacesuit and we trained underwater thousands of times.

---

[6] Hadfield is referring to the experiments being conducted by the scientists living aboard the space station. These experiments are literally teaching us about space and the universe.

[7] The expression "slammed shut" gives us the understanding that Hadfield's eye problem was unexpected, sudden, and dramatic.

[8] The word "goosh" is the sound that liquid makes when a large amount of it falls down.

[9] Hadfield is referring to the preparation work he did in training as being analogous to walking through spider webs to deal with spider phobia. This is covered in Lesson A.

And we don't just practice things going right, we practice things going wrong all the time, so that you are constantly walking through those spider webs. And not just underwater, but also in **virtual reality labs**[10] with the helmet and the gloves so you feel like it's realistic. So when you finally actually get outside on a spacewalk, it feels much different than it would if you just went out first time. And even if you're blinded, your natural, panicky reaction doesn't happen. Instead you kind of look around and go, "OK, I can't see, but I can hear, I can talk, **Scott Parazynski**[11] is out here with me. He could come over and help me." We actually practiced incapacitated crew rescue, so he could float me like a blimp and stuff me into the **airlock**[12] if he had to. I could find my own way back. It's not nearly as big a deal. And actually, if you keep on crying for a while, whatever that **gunk**[13] was that's in your eye starts to dilute and you can start to see again, and Houston, if you negotiate with them, they will let you then keep working. We finished everything on the spacewalk and when we came back inside, Jeff got some cotton batting and took the crusty stuff around my eyes, and

it turned out it was just the anti-fog, sort of a mixture of oil and soap, that got in my eye. And now we use **Johnson's No More Tears**,[14] which we probably should've been using right from the very beginning.

But the key to that is by looking at the difference between perceived danger and actual danger, where is the real risk? What is the real thing that you should be afraid of? Not just a generic fear of bad things happening. You can fundamentally change your reaction to things so that it allows you to go places and see things and do things that otherwise would be completely denied to you . . . where you can see the hardpan south of the Sahara, or you can see New York City in a way that is almost dreamlike, or the unconscious gingham of Eastern Europe fields or the Great Lakes as a collection of small puddles. You can see the fault lines of San Francisco and the way the water pours out under the bridge, just entirely different than any other way that you could have if you had not found a way to conquer your fear. You see a beauty that otherwise never would have happened. . . .

---

[10] A "virtual reality lab" is a room where computers create fake realities to test human reactions and skills in different situations.

[11] Scott Parazynski, Hadfield's partner on the spacewalk when he went blind, is an American astronaut who has been on over five shuttle flights.

[12] An "airlock" is a space with doors on either end in which the pressure is controlled so that a person can pass between two places with varying degrees of pressure.

[13] The term "gunk" is a colloquial one used to refer to substances that are sticky.

[14] "Johnson's No More Tears" is a brand of children's soap and shampoo that does not sting when it gets in the eyes.

Credits

11 Christian Ziegler/National Geographic Creative. **17** Xpacifica/National Geographic Creative.
23 ©Ociacia/Shutterstock.com. **29** Earth Welty/Aurora Photos. **35** Carl David Granback/National
Geographic Creative. **41** Aaron Huey/National Geographic Creative. **47** Mahmoud Zayyat/AFP/
Getty Images. **53** Krista Rossow/National Geographic Creative. **59** Cyril Ruoso/Minden Pictures.
65 Joey Schuster.

Acknowledgements

The Authors and Publisher would like to thank the following teaching professionals for their valuable
input during the development of this series:

Coleeta Paradise Abdullah, Certified Training Center; **Wilder Yesid Escobar Almeciga,**
Universidad El Bosque; **Tara Amelia Arntsen,** Northern State University; **Mei-ho Chiu,**
Soochow University; **Amy Cook,** Bowling Green State University; **Anthony Sean D'Amico,**
SDH Institute; **Mariel Doyenart,** Alianza Cultural Uruguay-Estados Unidos; **Raichle Farrelly,**
American University of Armenia; **Douglas E. Forster,** Japan Women's University; **Rosario
Giraldez,** Alianza Cultural Uruguay-Estados Unidos; **Floyd H. Graham III,** Kansai Gaidai
University; **Jay Klaphake,** Kyoto University of Foreign Studies; **Anthony G. Lavigne,** Kansai
Gaidai University; **Adriana Castañeda Londoño,** Centro Colombo Americano; **Alexandra
Dylan Lowe,** SUNY Westchester Community College; **Elizabeth Ortiz Lozada,** COPEI - COPOL
English Institute; **David Matijasevich,** Canadian Education College; **Jennie Popp,** Universidad
Andrés Bello; **Ubon Pun-ubon,** Sripatum University; **Yoko Sakurai,** Aichi University; **Michael J.
Sexton,** PSB Academy; **Jenay Seymour,** Hongik University; **Karenne Sylvester,** New College
Manchester; **Mark S. Turnoy; Hajime Uematsu,** Hirosaki University; **Nae-Dong Yang,** National
Taiwan University.